Reason To Write

Strategies for Success in Academic Writing

Low Intermediate

D0565721

Judy L. Miller
and
Robert F. Cohen

OXFORD

UNIVERSITY PRESS

OXFORD
UNIVERSITY PRESS

198 Madison Avenue
New York, NY 10016 USA

Great Clarendon Street
Oxford OX2 6DP England

Oxford New York

Auckland Cape Town Dar es Salaam
Hong Kong Karachi Kuala Lumpur Madrid
Melbourne Mexico City Nairobi New Delhi
Shanghai Taipei Toronto

With offices in

Argentina Austria Brazil Chile Czech Republic
France Greece Guatemala Hungary Italy Japan
Poland Portugal Singapore South Korea
Switzerland Thailand Turkey Ukraine Vietnam

OXFORD is a trademark of Oxford University Press.

ISBN: 978 0 19 436771 4

Copyright © 2001 Oxford University Press

Editorial Manager: Janet Aitchison
Senior Editor: Amy Cooper
Production Editor: Justin Hartung / Jeff Holt
Associate Editor: Kim Steiner
Art Director: Lynn Luchetti
Design Manager: Lynne Torrey
Designer: Gail de Luca / Jennifer Manzelli
Art Buyer: Elizabeth Blomster
Production Manager: Shanta Persaud
Production Coordinator: Eve Wong

Printing (last digit): 10

Printed in Hong Kong.

Illustrations by Barbara Bastian
Cover design by Silver Editions
Cover illustration by Rob Colvin
Realia by Annie Bissett, Maj-Britt Hagsted
The publishers would like to thank the following for their
permission to reproduce photographs:

W. Bokelberg/The Image Bank; Corbis/Bettmann; Culver
Pictures, Inc./SuperStock; National Portrait Gallery/
SuperStock; Jaime Abecasis/SuperStock; Underwood Photo
Archives/SuperStock; AP/Wide World Photos; Chris
Ranier/Corbis; Culver Pictures, Inc./SuperStock; Reuters
New Media, Inc./Corbis; Corbis-Royalty Free; Kristoffe
Gillette/Corbis/Sygma; Les Stone/Corbis/Sygma; Hulton-
Deutsch Collection/Corbis; Archivo Iconographico/Corbis;
Purchase, Emily Crane Chadbourne Bequest, 1972/
Metropolitan Museum of Art; Francis G. Mayer/Corbis;
Dallas and John Heaton/Corbis; Skip Nall/PhotoDisc; Steve
Chenn/Corbis; EyeWire Collection/EyeWire; James
Thurber/Barbara Hogenson; Brooks Kraft/Corbis/Sygma

*The publishers would also like to thank the following for
their help:*

"Little Boy who Could" from *Newsweek*, July 4. Copyright
© 1988 Newsweek, Inc. All rights reserved. Reprinted by
permission.

Life Expectancy Graph from *The New York Times*,
December 19, 1999. Copyright © 1999 The New York
Times, Inc. Reprinted by permission.

Excerpt from "How the Bean Saved Civilization" by
Umberto Eco (translated by William Weaver) from *New York
Times Magazine*, April 18, 1999. Reprinted by permission of
Umberto Eco and William Weaver.

Excerpts from *The House on Mango Street*. Copyright ©
1984 by Sandra Cisneros. Published by Vintage Books, a
division of Random House, Inc., New York, and in
hardcover by Alfred A. Knopf in 1994. Reprinted by
permission of Susan Bergholz Literary Services, New York.
All rights reserved.

"10G Can't Tempt Cabby" by Austin Penner from New York
Daily News, February 1, 1988. Copyright © 1998 New York
Daily News, L.P. Reprinted with permission.

"The Litle Girl and the Wolf" from *Fables for Our time*.
Copyright © 1940 by James Thurber. Copyright © renewed
1968 by Helen Thurber and Rosemary A. Thurber. Reprinted
by arrangement with Rosemary A. Thurber and The Barbara
Hogenson Agency. All rights reserved.

"The Princess and the Bowling Ball" from *The Stinky
Cheeseman and Other Fairly Stupid Tales* by Jon Scieszka.
Copyright © 1992 by Jon Scieszka. Used by permission of
Viking Penguin, a division of Penguin Putnam, Inc.

"The New Frog Prince," All Rights Reserved, Recycled
Paper Greetings, Inc. Reprinted by permission.

"What I Have Lived For" from *Autobiography of Bertrand
Russell*, Bertrand Russell. Routledge, Ltd., (U.K.) 1978, and
The Bertrand Russell Peace Foundation.

Trademarks used in this text are the sole property of their
respective owners.

AUTHOR ACKNOWLEDGEMENTS

To our wonderful editor, Amy Cooper, we owe our deepest gratitude. It is because of her confidence in our work that this series was launched and brought to fruition. The warmth, intelligence, and professionalism that she brought to our collaboration have made it a privilege to know her and work with her.

Our sincere thanks also go to Elizabeth Blomster, Gail de Luca, Justin Hartung, Jeff Holt, Jennifer Manzelli, Kim Steiner, and Lynne Torrey for their essential contributions to this project.

We thank our colleagues at the American Language Program at Columbia University and the Department of Language and Cognition at Eugenio María de Hostos Community College for their professional support and friendship.

Finally, we remember our students, from whom we continue to learn every day and who remain in our hearts our true teachers.

In loving memory of my father, Ben Miller, violinist, musicians' union stalwart, generous and loving soul.

Judy L. Miller

To my mother, Lillian Kumock Cohen, who remains to this day my true alma mater.

Robert F. Cohen

REASON TO WRITE

STRATEGIES FOR SUCCESS IN ACADEMIC WRITING

Introduction

Writing in one's own language is difficult enough. Imagine how much more daunting a task it is for students to write in a second language. If the weight of writer's block does not inhibit their impulse to move forward with a writing assignment, their insecurity with the language and its particular writing culture sometimes will make them stare at the blank page with trepidation. ESL/EFL teachers thus have a dual challenge: Not only must they help the most reticent and timid writers overcome a potentially crippling writing phobia, but they must also instill in their students the confidence needed to translate their thoughts into correct and acceptable English. The communicative approach that we use in the *Reason to Write* series will help teachers achieve this end.

Even though the writing product is an expression of one's individuality and personality, it is important to remember that writing is also a social endeavor, a way of communicating with others, informing them, persuading them, and debating with them. In our attempt to provide guidelines, strategies, and practice in writing for university, college, community college, and high school ESL/EFL students preparing for the academic demands of all disciplines in higher education, we want students to realize that they are not writing in a vacuum. They have a voice, and what they write will elicit a reaction from others. In our books writing is, therefore, an active communicative/social process involving discussion, interaction with teachers, group work, pair work, and peer evaluation. Through these collaborative experiences, students come to recognize their unique strengths while they cultivate their critical-thinking skills and become more effective writers.

Content-based themes that speak to both the hearts and minds of students are the key to realizing our goal. Writing can develop only where there is meaning; it cannot be an empty exercise in form. And meaning cannot be understood unless students are given intellectually challenging and emotionally appealing material that generates their enthusiasm. Because all instruction in grammar, vocabulary, and rhetorical styles is presented in relation to a theme, each unit provides a seamless path from reading to thinking to writing, from the preparatory stages of writing to the completion of a final written composition. Working with one theme, the whole class experiences the same problem or issue at the same time, and students benefit from the security of shared discussion and exploration. As a result, writers are not left to suffer alone with the blank page. At the same time, students are given several writing options within each theme so that there is ample opportunity for individual expression.

Content-based themes also encourage the kind of critical thinking that students are expected to do across the curriculum in a college or university. Because many English-language learners may lack some of the analytical skills needed to do academic work, we provide them with experience in analyzing ideas, making inferences, supporting opinions, understanding points of view, and writing for different audiences. As students "reason to write," they practice the skills and strategies that are vital for academic success, and they have an opportunity to write on a wide variety of themes that reflect the academic curriculum.

There are five main sections in each unit.

I. Fluency Practice: Freewriting

All units begin with an unstructured writing task in which students can freely express their thoughts and share them with a partner, without worrying about grammar or spelling. In this section, students explore the theme of the unit by drawing on their own knowledge and ideas. As a result, they enter subsequent discussions with more self-assurance.

II. Reading for Writing

In order to develop as a writer, one must be a reader. Therefore, each unit contains a provocative reading passage followed by a series of writing activities that culminate in the main writing task of the unit. In this section, students consider the meaning of the reading and they work with the vocabulary and syntactic forms needed for discussing and writing.

III. Prewriting Activities

This section prepares the students for the main writing task by developing their interpretive skills. They must "read between the lines," infer the motives of the individuals in various scenarios, and write from different points of view. They are also asked to write short opinions of their own. As they complete these small writing tasks, students give and receive immediate feedback through ongoing dialogue with a partner or group, building confidence for the main writing task in the next section.

IV. Structured Writing Focus

When students reach the main writing task, they realize that all their work in previous sections has prepared them for this central writing assignment. Because we feel that students should be given choices, we have provided an alternative writing task.

In this section of the unit, students are guided through a series of steps that will lead to the successful completion of the writing task. In this first book of the series, students learn the rudiments of writing a well-developed paragraph. They learn how to organize a coherent paragraph as they practice writing topic sentences and concluding sentences and provide the necessary support for these statements. They learn to perfect these skills by performing tasks as varied as interviewing and writing about a classmate, writing about someone they admire, identifying an indispensable invention, writing a letter to the editor, explaining a process, analyzing a business problem, describing a place, and writing a story. In the last unit, we offer a preview of what comes next in the learning process. We show students how they will eventually weave one paragraph into a larger composition consisting of several paragraphs. "Writing an Essay" is therefore introduced in the last unit, giving the students a vision of our future goals in this series—the focus in the second book is on writing a well-developed essay.

To give students the support they need to accomplish the writing tasks, we provide a model for them to follow. The model is on a topic that is similar to the writing topic. Students then work through the brainstorming process and do exercises that help them prepare a first draft. After writing their first draft, they read it to a partner or a small group of students. In this way, peer evaluation becomes a regular part of the writing process and the class becomes a "writing workshop" in which the writing process is demystified and students learn how to look critically at their own work. Our guidelines for peer work ensure that this is a positive experience, a prelude but not a substitute for feedback from the teacher.

After writing a second draft, students are ready to proofread their work. At this point, the unit focuses on grammar. Students work through various editing exercises that focus on at least one grammar point that is central to the particular writing task and on another grammar point that is a general stumbling block for students at this level. After completing these grammar exercises and editing their second draft, students are ready to write their final draft.

V. Additional Writing Opportunities

We believe that students can perfect their writing skills only by writing a great deal. Therefore, in this section we give them the opportunity to write on a wide variety of additional stimulating topics. However, this time they are writing without our step-by-step guidance. As students learn to avail themselves of this additional writing practice in each unit, they will eventually develop the skills and confidence they need to become independent writers.

In conclusion, the *Reason to Write* series represents our effort to integrate the insights of whole language learning and writing workshops across the curriculum at the college level. These books were also written with the knowledge that no textbook can come to life and be effective without the creative contributions of the teachers and students who use it. We hope that you and your students will develop a strong connection with the material in this book and thus form a bond with us as you explore the writing process. We would appreciate any suggestions or comments you may have. You can write to us in care of Oxford University Press, ESL Department, 198 Madison Avenue, New York, New York 10016-4314.

Judy L. Miller and Robert F. Cohen

CONTENTS

1 GETTING ACQUAINTED

WRITING ABOUT SOMEONE YOU INTERVIEW

In this unit you will practice:
- asking questions
- taking notes
- writing a paragraph

Editing focus:
- capital letters
- simple present tense
- prepositions
- singular and plural nouns
- adverbs of frequency

I Fluency Practice: Freewriting

What is your name? Does it have a special meaning? Were you named after someone? If so, do you know that person? Who chose your name? Are you happy with your name? Have you ever had a nickname?

Write for ten minutes about your name. What does it tell about you? Try to express yourself as well as you can. Don't worry about mistakes. Share your writing with a partner.

1

II ▸ Reading for Writing

JONATHAN HARKER'S JOURNAL

I heard a heavy step and the great door opened. There stood an old man dressed all in black.

"Welcome to my house."

His face was strong, very strong. He had a high forehead. His eyebrows were very massive, almost meeting over the nose, with bushy hair. The mouth, as far as I could see under the white mustache, was fixed and cruel with sharp, white teeth. His ears were pointed and he was very pale and white. Strange to say, there were hairs in the center of his palm. As he leaned over me, a horrible feeling of nausea came over me. His hand was as cold as ice.

"Enter of your own free will," he said.

"You speak English very well," I said.

"Alas,[1] I know your language only through books. I know the grammar and the words, but yet I don't know how to speak them. You will stay with me a while, so that I may learn English intonation.[2] Tell me when I make an error, even the smallest, in my speaking."

What manner of man is this? Or what manner of creature in the shape of a man? I feel the dread[3] of this horrible place overcoming me. I am in fear, terrible fear, and there is no escape for me. I am surrounded by terrors that I dare not think of.

"Count Dracula?"

He bowed. "I am Dracula."

From *Dracula* by Bram Stoker

---

[1]*Alas:* unhappily
[2]*intonation:* pronunciation
[3]*dread:* fear

A. General Understanding

Answer these questions in your own words. Share your answers with a partner.

1. What is strange about the Count's appearance?

   _____

   _____

2. What does Count Dracula say he wants from Harker?

   _____

   _____

B. Words and Ideas

1. Dracula: Yesterday, Today, and Tomorrow

Look at these pictures from different film versions of the story of Dracula. Circle the one you like best. Then explain your answer to a partner.

a.   b.    c.

2. Open for Discussion

Discuss these questions in a small group.

1. Have you seen film versions of the Dracula story? If so, which one did you like best?

2. Why are stories about vampires and witches so popular?

3. Dracula's favorite victims are women. Is this an important element in the story?

4. What is your favorite horror story or horror movie?

5. Do you think there is a danger in reading these stories or watching these movies? Why or why not?

3. Famous People

Match these pictures of famous people with the descriptions below.

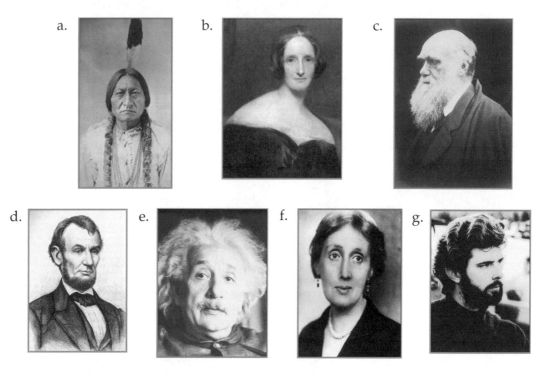

a.   b.   c.

d.   e.   f.   g.

Descriptions

___ 1. He is a thin man with a beard but no mustache. His hair is dark, and it is cut short.

___ 2. He is an old man with a wrinkled face and long, dark hair made into two braids.

___ 3. She has big dark eyes and a very high forehead. Her lips are thin, and her nose is long and straight. She has a long neck and sloping shoulders.

___ 4. He is an old man with a long white beard. He has thick, white eyebrows but not much hair.

___ 5. He has wild, curly hair and a mustache. There is a dimple in his chin.

Write your own descriptions for the remaining two people.

___ 6. _____

___ 7. _____

Who are these people? Turn to page 168 to find out.

III ◆ Prewriting Activities

Getting to Know You

1. Asking *Yes/No* Questions

With forms of *be*, put the verb before the subject:

Are   **you**   sometimes homesick?

VERB   SUBJECT

With all other verbs, follow this pattern:
auxiliary *do* + subject + base form of the verb

Do   **you**   **like**   Chinese food?

DO   SUBJECT   BASE FORM

Using the descriptions below, ask your classmates questions about themselves.
Write only one name on each line. Try to write a different name on each line.

Find someone who . . .

_____ is sometimes homesick.

_____ likes Chinese food.

_____ drinks coffee every day.

_____ is married.

_____ wears glasses.

_____ dislikes American food.

_____ buys a doughnut every day.

_____ often reads a newspaper.

_____ is always nervous about speaking English.

_____ lives with a roommate.

_____ has two brothers.

_____ smokes cigarettes.

_____ uses e-mail all the time.

_____ always tells the truth.

_____ listens to rap music.

_____ likes to study English.

_____ likes to paint.

_____ watches TV in English.

_____ loves sports.

_____ dislikes living in the city.

2. Forming Adjective Clauses with *Who*

An adjective clause is a group of words that acts like an adjective. It tells you more about a person or thing.

Maria is in my class, and she drinks coffee every day.
Maria, **who is in my class,** drinks coffee every day.
       ADJECTIVE CLAUSE

Choose five people in your class. Write a sentence about each of them based on information from your list. Here are more examples:

Byong Woo, who sits next to me, is married.
Sergei, who loves pizza, is a new friend.
Yumiko, who wears glasses, has beautiful dark hair.

1. _____

2. _____

3. _____

4. _____

5. _____

3. Forming *Wh-* Questions: *Who? What? Where? When? Why? How?*

With forms of *be*, put the question word first, and then verb + subject:

What	**is**	**your name?**
QUESTION WORD	VERB	SUBJECT

With all other verbs, follow this pattern:
question word + auxiliary *do* + subject + base form of the verb

Where	**do**	**you**	**live?**
QUESTION WORD	DO	SUBJECT	BASE FORM

Make these cues into questions.

1. when / birthday ?

   <u>When is your birthday?</u>

2. where / come from ?

   <u>Where do you come from?</u>

3. how big / family ?

   _____

4. where / work ?

   _____

5. what / hobbies ?

   _____

6. what / do / on weekends ?

   _____

7. what / favorite book or movie ?

   _____

8. why / like / this book or movie ?

   _____

Add two more questions of your own.

9. _____

10. _____

4. Interviewing Your Partner

Ask a partner questions, and take notes about the answers. You can use the questions on page 7 and add more questions of your own.

Questions	Your Partner's Answers

IV Structured Writing Focus

YOUR TASK

Write a paragraph telling the class about your partner.

A. Starting to Write

Organizing Your Notes

Look back at the notes from the interview with your partner on page 8. Choose the most important and interesting things to write about your partner. Remember to include:

- a brief physical description: tall with dark hair—smiling eyes—dimples

- facts about the person: 28 years old—math teacher in China

- the person's feelings and opinions: very homesick—mother's food hates hamburgers and fries

_____

_____

_____

_____

_____

_____

_____

B. Preparing the First Draft

1. How to Write a Paragraph

A paragraph is a group of sentences about the same topic. In academic writing, a paragraph usually consists of five to seven sentences. The first sentence gives the general idea of the whole paragraph.

2. Presentation

Read the following two versions of student writing. Which one do you think is the acceptable academic version? How many differences can you find in the two versions?

My amazing partner

My partner is a gorgeous woman. She is small and delicate
with a gentle smile.
When I saw her for the first time, I thought she was just cute and silent
, but I realize that she has charm and an artistic
character.
Her name is Yoko, and she has parents and a younger sister in Tokyo.
she sometimes misses her family, friends, and especially her dog, Coco
. Yoko, who majors in film, likes to take pictures all the time.
I hope we have a good relationship in class.

My Amazing Partner

My partner is a gorgeous woman. She is small and delicate with a gentle smile. When I saw her for the first time, I thought she was just cute and silent, but I realize that she has charm and an artistic character. Her name is Yoko, and she has parents and a younger sister in Tokyo. She sometimes misses her family, friends, and especially her dog, Coco. Yoko, who majors in film, likes to take pictures all the time. I hope we have a good relationship in class.

*Review your notes and write a **first draft** of your paragraph about your partner. This time write complete sentences.*

C. Revising the First Draft

Read your paragraph to the person you interviewed. Ask the person for a photo or other material that you can include with your final draft to help people get to know your partner.

QUESTIONS TO DISCUSS WITH THE INTERVIEWEE:

1. Did I get all the facts right?
2. Are all the names and places spelled correctly?
3. Are there more examples or facts to add?
4. Did I hurt your feelings by mistake?

*After talking with your interviewee and thinking about your paragraph, write a **second draft** that includes all the additions and changes. Make sure you choose a good title and an interesting first sentence.*

D. Editing the Second Draft

After you have written a second draft, proofread your work to find any errors and correct them. These guidelines and exercises should help.

1. Adverbs and Expressions of Frequency

Study these sentences:

Flora is **always** on time.
Jaime **always** arrives on time.

Maurice does his homework **every day.**
Every day Maurice does his homework.

Adverbs of Frequency	Expressions of Frequency
always	once a month
never	twice a day
often	every morning
sometimes	

1. With the verb *be*, the adverb of frequency goes **after** the verb.

2. With all other verbs, the adverb of frequency goes **before** the verb.

3. Expressions of frequency can go **at the beginning** or **at the end** of a sentence.

Unscramble the following sentences and compare your answers with a partner's.

1. every listens music to Yumiko morning

   Yumiko listens to music every morning.

2. always speaking nervous is Eduardo about English

   _____

3. Alexander American food eats never

   _____

4. week tennis Ilana twice plays a

   _____

5. homesick Hyun-Jin weekend often is on the

   _____

6. tells Stavros truth sometimes the

   _____

2. Proofreading Practice

Find the six errors in this paragraph and correct them.

My partner is from the Dominican republic. His name is Wilson

, and he have a wife and a little daughter. He arrived here on september

and worked for six month.

Capital Letters
Names of people, countries, organizations, nationalities, months,
and days of the week, and the first and all important words in titles.

Prepositions of Place and Date

He lives **on** Maple Avenue.   She arrived **in** April.

He lives **at** 43 Maple Avenue.   She arrived **on** April 2, 2001.

Simple Present Tense

I have	We have
You have	They have
He has*	
She has*	

*The third person singular in the present tense usually has an *s*.

Singular and Plural Nouns

book ➤ book**s**	Add *s*.
berry ➤ berr**ies**	Change the *y* to *i* and add *es*.
boss ➤ boss**es**	For endings with *ch, s, sh, x,* or *z*, add *es*.
wife ➤ wi**ves**	Drop the *f* or *fe* and add *ves*.
hero ➤ hero**es**	For endings with *o*, sometimes add *es* and
piano ➤ piano**s**	sometimes add *s*. (Consult a dictionary.)

Find the ten errors in this paragraph and correct them.

I would like you to meet Steven. Steven is an English name, but he is chinese. His real name is Zhaomeng. He is 32 year old and has visited many countrys. He has two sister and one brother. He work at a financial company at 42nd Street, and he also studies english. He like to play golf, exercise, and sing. He came here in may 1999, and he thought people didn't look friendly. But three day later, he felt better when he met his cousin. Now he has a good career.

E. Preparing the Final Draft
REMINDERS FOR PRESENTATION

- Center the title.
- Begin the first word and each important word in the title with a capital letter.
- Indent to begin a paragraph.
- Begin each sentence with a capital letter.
- Don't use a new line for each sentence. Write one sentence after the other.
- Never begin a new line with a comma or a period.
- Skip a line (or double-space) so that your teachers can make corrections easily.

Reread your second draft and correct any errors in presentation or grammar. Put a check (✓) in each space as you edit for the points below. Then write your corrected final version. Add a photo if you wish.

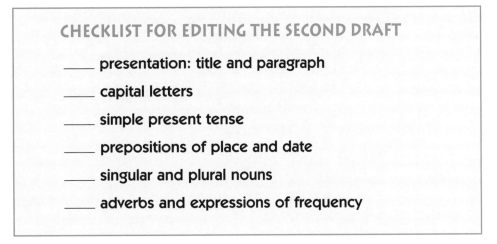

CHECKLIST FOR EDITING THE SECOND DRAFT

_____ **presentation: title and paragraph**

_____ **capital letters**

_____ **simple present tense**

_____ **prepositions of place and date**

_____ **singular and plural nouns**

_____ **adverbs and expressions of frequency**

V Additional Writing Opportunities

Choose one of the following topics and write a paragraph.

1. Why are horror stories so popular? Which one is the most frightening in your opinion? How do you feel when you read or see such a story? Explain your answer.

2. Describe your physical appearance. What do you like about the way you look? What things do you want to change?

3. What do you do every day? Describe a normal day in your life and how you feel about it.

4. Did your first impression of a person ever change when you got to know the person better? Was your first impression good or bad? How did it change?

5. "What's in a name? A rose by any other name would smell as sweet."

   This quote is from *Romeo and Juliet* by William Shakespeare. What do you think it means?

   Do you think names are very important or not? Did you ever change any part of your name?

6. Interview a friend, a member of your family, or a teacher about what he or she does in his or her free time. Then write about that person in a paragraph.

2 WHO IS A HERO?

WRITING ABOUT SOMEONE YOU ADMIRE

In this unit you will practice:
- organizing ideas
- choosing a topic sentence
- choosing a concluding sentence

Editing focus:
- connectors: *and, but*
- count and noncount nouns

I Fluency Practice: Freewriting

Did you ever help anyone who was in trouble? Was it a family member or a friend? a classmate in school? a neighbor? a stranger? Did the story have a happy ending? Did someone ever help you? Who was it? What was the result?

Write for ten minutes about how you helped someone or about how someone helped you. Try to express yourself as well as you can. Don't worry about mistakes. Share your writing with a partner.

Here are some expressions you may want to use:

He was grateful for my help.
She was thankful for my help.
I thanked them for their help.

II ▸ Reading for Writing

THE LITTLE BOY WHO COULD

(from *Newsweek*)

Rocky Lyons never tired of hearing about "The Little Engine That Could."[1] Last Halloween[2] his parents found out just how much the story meant to him, and to them. Rocky's Dad, Marty Lyons, was away playing football for the New York Jets. His Mom, Kelly, was driving home through rural Alabama with five-year-old Marty, Jr., known as Rocky, asleep beside her. Suddenly, their pickup truck hit a huge pothole.[3] It bounced out, flipped over, and fell down a hill to the bottom of a forty-foot ravine.[4] "I had blood all over my face and in my eyes, and I thought I was blind," Mrs. Lyons recalls. "I told Rocky to get away because I thought the truck might explode."

The boy obeyed—and then ran back to try to pull her from the wrecked car. "Come on, Mom. I can help you get up the hill. I can push," he said. All of 4 feet and 2 inches and 55 pounds, Rocky began to push his mother up the slope.[5] "Gosh Mom, I bet you weigh a thousand pounds," he said. Even in pain, Mrs. Lyons had to smile at that. But halfway up the hill, she told her son she could go no farther. "Oh, Mom, think of the little train: I think I can, I think I can, I think I can. That's what it said," he insisted. They started up again. Finally, they crawled to the highway, where a passing car took them to the hospital. Rocky's mother had two broken shoulders and needed 70 stitches to close the wounds on her face. Without her son's perseverance, she's sure she would have bled to death.

---

[1]*"The Little Engine That Could"* is a children's story about a little train that had to go up a mountain. The train said, "I think I can, I think I can" to get the courage. Finally, it succeeded.
[2]*Halloween:* October 31; holiday when children dress up as ghosts and witches, for example, and ask for candy
[3]*pothole:* a large hole in the road
[4]*ravine:* a valley with steep, high walls of rock
[5]*slope:* an incline, not flat land

A. General Understanding

Choose the correct ending for each sentence.

1. The main idea of the story is that
    a. Rocky wasn't hurt in the accident.
    b. Rocky saved his mother's life.
    c. Rocky's mother died in the accident.

2. Rocky and his mother were in a truck that
    a. crashed into another car.
    b. ran out of gas.
    c. went off the road.

3. Rocky and his mother had to crawl up to the road because
    a. Rocky was hurt.
    b. Rocky's mother was bleeding a lot.
    c. the car exploded.

4. Rocky's father
    a. lives in New York.
    b. is dead.
    c. is a professional athlete.

5. Rocky is an unusual hero because
    a. he is a child who saved an adult.
    b. he survived an accident.
    c. he needed 70 stitches.

6. "The Little Engine That Could" is important to this story because
    a. Rocky was tired of it.
    b. Rocky could read it himself.
    c. it inspired Rocky to make a great effort.

B. Words and Ideas

A Mother's Story

Use these words to fill in the blanks in the letter.

crawl   flipped   recall   wreck
explode   perseverance   rural   wounds

Dear Mom,

　　You won't believe what happened to Rocky and me this week.

My pickup truck hit a pothole in the road, and it _____

　　　　　　　　　　　　　　　　　　　　　　　　　　1

over and fell down a hill. Luckily, my truck didn't _____

　　　　　　　　　　　　　　　　　　　　　　　　　　2

and burn up. I was hurt very badly, and I couldn't walk or think

clearly. Your grandson and I had to _____ up a hill to

　　　　　　　　　　　　　　　　　　3

get back to the road. As you know, we live in a _____

　　　　　　　　　　　　　　　　　　　　　　　　4

area and not in a city. There aren't many people here, but finally a

car came by. I can remember every minute of this story, and I can

_____ every detail because I am so proud of my son.

5

I needed 70 stitches to close the _____ on my face,

　　　　　　　　　　　　　　　　　　6

but don't worry. I'm OK. My pickup is a complete _____.

　　　　　　　　　　　　　　　　　　　　　　　　　　7

We have to buy a new one, but at least we are safe and alive,

thanks to this child. Rocky is a hero because he had

_____ and helped me keep going. Can you believe it?

8

His father is very proud of him too.

　　Be well and we'll see you next week.

　　　　　　　　　　　　　　　Your loving daughter,

　　　　　　　　　　　　　　　Kelly

III Prewriting Activities

Describing Heroes

1. What Do You Think?

What are some qualities of a hero? Look at the adjectives in the table below and put a check (✓) in the column that best expresses your opinion. Then circle the characteristic you think is the most important. Discuss your answers with a partner.

A HERO IS . . .

	Yes	No	Maybe
brave			
unselfish			
happy			
intelligent			
shy			
proud			
confident			
reliable			
rich			
loyal			
popular			

2. Open for Discussion

Discuss these questions in a small group.

1. What kinds of people do you admire?

2. A hero is someone who has made a difference in someone else's life. Do you agree or disagree with this statement?

3. Why do so many people admire sports heroes? Are they good heroes for young people?

4. Do you think film stars make good heroes? Choose an example and discuss why or why not.

5. There are stories about heroes who are born rich and help the poor, and there are heroes who are poor and become rich. Can you think of some examples? Which kind of hero do you like, and why?

IV ▸ Structured Writing Focus

YOUR TASK

Write about someone you admire. You can choose someone you know very well, such as a family member, a friend, or a teacher, or you can choose a famous person, such as a national leader, a scientist, or an artist.

ALTERNATIVE TASK: **If you have no hero, explain why not. You may want to consider why political and military leaders are not heroes for many people.**

A. Starting to Write

1. Brainstorming

Brainstorming means writing down all your ideas just as they come to you. You do not have to write complete sentences or worry about grammar.

Write some notes about your partner.

Identify the person.	my sister, younger
What are this person's **characteristics**?	smarter than I am
Why is this person **special**?	the kindest heart

_____

_____

_____

_____

_____

_____

_____

2. Organizing Your Ideas

Look at these brainstorming notes that a student prepared before writing a paragraph about Martin Luther King.

WHY AMERICANS ADMIRE MARTIN LUTHER KING

NOTES	PARAGRAPH
1 important leader ~~born in Atlanta, Georgia~~ 6 shot in 1968/workers' strike 7 protests after his death 8 national holiday 2 equal rights movement 3 nonviolence 4 Nobel Peace Prize 1964, age 35 ~~met his wife at college~~ 5 never showed he was afraid	Martin Luther King was never elected president, and he never made a billion dollars, but he was an important leader. He led a peaceful movement for equal rights in the United States. He used nonviolence as a way of convincing people to change. For that, he won the Nobel Peace Prize in 1964 at the age of 35. He knew that there were people who wanted to kill him, but he never showed that he was afraid. In 1968 he was helping a workers' strike in the South when he was shot by a racist. The whole country was shocked. There were protests in black neighborhoods all over the nation. Today, he is honored by his country with a national holiday on the third Monday in January. In remembering him, we remember these words from the Declaration of Independence: "All men are created equal."

In organizing the paragraph about Martin Luther King, the writer left out information about King's birthplace and where he met his wife. This information is not important to explain why we admire King. Then the writer organized the other notes chronologically, in the order in which the events happened.

Now look back at your brainstorming notes and organize them before you write. Be sure to leave out any points that are not essential to the main idea.

B. Preparing the First Draft

1. The Topic Sentence

The topic sentence is usually the first sentence in a paragraph. It gives the main idea of the whole paragraph.

2. Choosing a Topic Sentence and a Concluding Sentence

Read this paragraph about Martin Luther King. Then choose the best topic sentence from the choices that follow.

HOW MARTIN LUTHER KING CHANGED

_____

_____

He was born in the American South where black and white people were kept apart by law. Like his father, he became a Baptist minister. At first, he believed that only revolution could convince whites to give black people a chance in the South. Then, he met some Christian anti-war groups working against violence and racism. These groups had both black and white members. Martin Luther King read a lot about nonviolence and Christian love. He began to change his mind about violence. His first job was in Montgomery, Alabama. In that city, African Americans were protesting against discrimination on the buses. Martin Luther King was their minister. He saw how brave the black people were in their peaceful protests. He also saw how some white people came to support them and how the protesters won a victory. He realized that nonviolent protest could start a mass movement. He believed that such a movement could make important changes in the United States. Later, he defended the rights of poor people and workers and tried to convince the government to stop the war in Vietnam. He remained true to his vision of peaceful change. In a world of violence, Martin Luther King changed himself before he tried to change others.

Put a check (✓) next to the best topic sentence.

_____ a. Martin Luther King was born in 1929.

_____ b. Martin Luther King was a hero because he had the courage to change.

_____ c. Martin Luther King was a hero.

_____ d. The person I admire most is Martin Luther King.

Read this paragraph about everyday heroes. Then choose the best topic sentence and concluding sentence from the choices that follow.

HEROES OF EVERYDAY LIFE

_____

_____

When my parents were children, they lived through the Great Depression in the 1930s. There was no work and no money, but both my parents always loved music, and that helped them through hard times. My mother became a pianist, and my father became a violinist. When they grew up and got married, they had to face World War II. My father went into the army to fight in a war where many people died. My mother followed him across the country from one army base to another. She, too, got a job with the army. After the war, there were no houses for the ex-soldiers and sometimes no jobs, but my parents were full of hope. My mother grew up in an unhappy home. Her parents were always fighting and never paid attention to her. She promised herself that when she had children of her own, she would be a warm and loving mother. She and my father built a home full of love for each other and for their children. They insisted that my sister and I go to the best universities, and they worked very hard to pay for our education. Both my parents have spent their lives playing music and teaching it to others. My father earned his living and the respect of his colleagues without ever hurting another human being.

_____

_____

Put a check (✓) next to the best topic sentence.

_____ a. My parents are my heroes.

_____ b. My parents had a hard life.

_____ c. My parents lived through good times and bad but remained moral people, loving parents, and dedicated musicians.

_____ d. I am going to tell you about the people I admire most.

Put a check (✓) next to the best concluding sentence.

_____ a. That's why I admire my parents.

_____ b. My parents were brave and did many things to help others.

_____ c. My parents are heroes who are devoted to their family and others around them.

_____ d. My parents are getting older now, and they sometimes have a hard time doing everything they want to do.

PARTS OF A GOOD PARAGRAPH:

- a topic sentence: My parents lived through good times and bad but remained moral people, loving parents, and dedicated musicians.

- lots of examples: They built a home full of love.
  They never hurt anyone.
  They spent their lives playing and teaching music.

- a concluding sentence: My parents are heroes who are devoted to their family and others around them.

A **concluding sentence** reminds the reader of the main idea given in the topic sentence.

Look at the concluding sentences in "How Martin Luther King Changed" and "Heroes of Everyday Life." Consider these questions:

1. Does the concluding sentence repeat the exact words of the topic sentence?

2. Are the ideas of the concluding sentence and the topic sentence very similar?

*Review your notes and write a **first draft** of your paragraph about someone you admire. This time write complete sentences. Try to use some of the vocabulary you have practiced in this unit.*

C. Revising the First Draft

Read your paragraph to a partner.

CHECKLIST FOR REVISING THE FIRST DRAFT

When you listen to a partner's paragraph and discuss your own, keep these questions in mind:

1. Is it clear why the writer admires this person?

2. Do you need more information to explain the facts?

3. Did you enjoy learning more about this person?

4. Did the writer choose effective topic and concluding sentences?

5. Is there an interesting title?

---

*Now write a **second draft** that includes all the additions and changes.*

D. Editing the Second Draft

After you have written a second draft, proofread your work to find any errors and correct them. These guidelines and exercises should help.

1. The Connectors *and* and *but*

Use *and* to connect two sentences that have similar ideas.

Incorrect grammar:
Mrs. Lyons told Rocky to leave the area, he obeyed.

Correct but poor style:
Mrs. Lyons told Rocky to leave the area. He obeyed.

Correct and good style:
Mrs. Lyons told Rocky to leave the area, **and** he obeyed.

Use *but* to connect two sentences that have contrasting or opposite ideas.

Incorrect grammar:
Mrs. Lyons wanted Rocky to stay away from the truck, he ran back to her.

Correct but poor style:
Mrs. Lyons wanted Rocky to stay away from the truck. He ran back to her.

Correct and good style:
Mrs. Lyons wanted Rocky to stay away from the truck, **but** he ran back to her.

Read these sentences about Martin Luther King. Fill in the blanks with and *or* but. *Compare your answers with a partner's.*

1. Martin Luther King died more than 30 years ago, _____ we haven't forgotten his work.

2. King is considered an American hero, _____ he is the only African American to have a national holiday in his memory.

3. King asked people to protest in peaceful ways, _____ he was given the Nobel Peace Prize for his nonviolent movement.

4. King was an intelligent man who knew his life was in danger, _____ he wouldn't give up trying to make life better.

Using and *or* but, *rewrite each pair of sentences below to make one sentence. Remember to replace the period at the end of the first sentence with a comma. Compare your answers with a partner's.*

1. King had white friends when he was little. Their father soon stopped letting them play with him.

   King had white friends when he was little, **but** their father

   soon stopped letting them play with him.

2. King wanted to hate every white person. His father told him he must love instead of hate.

   _____

   _____

3. He protested with nonviolent marches. He established the Southern Christian Leadership Conference in order to organize these demonstrations.

   _____

   _____

4. Many people were pleased when King won the Nobel Peace Prize. His ideas weren't accepted by some violent civil rights activists.

   _____

   _____

5. Martin Luther King lived for peace. A violent act caused his death.

   _____

   _____

Count and Noncount Nouns

Count nouns are the names of separate objects, people, and ideas that we can count. Count nouns have both a **singular** and a **plural** form. You can say *one book*, *two books*, *three books*, etc. The plural form usually ends with -*s* or -*es*.

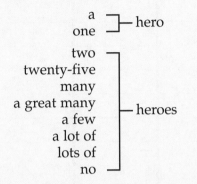

Noncount nouns are the names of materials, liquids, and other things that we do not count as separate objects. Noncount nouns have only a **singular** form. You cannot say *one information, two informations*. You must say *a little information, a lot of information*.

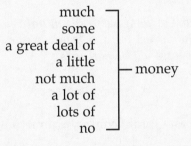

Different languages may count things in different ways. Some common words that are noncount nouns in English are:

advice	money
furniture	news
information	research
knowledge	weather
luggage	

Some words can be both count and noncount:*

Count:	**Noncount:**
I have to write **two papers** for English.	I'd like **some paper.**
We'll have **two black coffees**, please.	Would you like **some coffee**?

* To be sure about whether a noun is count or noncount, use a good dictionary.

With a partner, decide whether these nouns are count or noncount. Put a check (✓) in the correct column.

	Count	Noncount
courage		✓
deeds		
help		
money		
people		
perseverance		
happiness		
projects		
scholarships		
knowledge		

*Read the paragraph below. Decide if the words in **bold** print are count or noncount. Then choose the correct word or words in parentheses to fill in the blanks. Compare your answers with a partner's.*

OPRAH'S PROJECTS

TV talk-show host Oprah Winfrey wants to help people. One of her *(much, many, a few)* _____ **projects** is to help
1
poor students who need money for their college education.

Recently, she collected *(a great deal of, a great many, a few)*

_____ **money** to give *(fifty, much, a great deal of)*
2

_____ $25,000 **scholarships.** *(Much, Many, A little)*
3

_____ **people** from all over America give to her
4

projects. You don't have to be rich. Even people with *(little, few, not many)*

_____ **money** of their own can
5

participate in her projects for *(a little, a few, not much)*

_____ **dollars.** Oprah gives you *(a great deal of, a
6

great many, a few)* _____ **information** about her
7

projects on her TV program. You can gain *(a few, a lot of, many)*

_____ **knowledge** about the people who deserve

(not many, a little, a few) _____ **help.** You don't need

(much, many, few) _____ **courage** to do the right

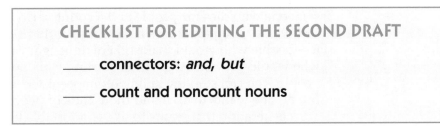

thing. All you need is *(many, few, lots of)*

_____ **perseverance** and a

big heart. Giving to others brings

(a great deal of, a few, many) _____

happiness to everyone.

E. Preparing the Final Draft

Reread your second draft and correct any errors you find. Put a check (✓) in each space as you edit for the points below. Then write your corrected final version.

CHECKLIST FOR EDITING THE SECOND DRAFT

_____ **connectors:** *and, but*

_____ **count and noncount nouns**

Additional Writing Opportunities

Choose one of the following topics and write a paragraph.

1. Young people often think that athletes and film stars are heroes. Why do they think that? Do you agree or disagree? Why?

2. Rocky Lyons is a hero, and so is Martin Luther King. How are these two heroes similar? How are they different?

3. People seem to love superheroes in movies and in comic books. For example, Superman is very popular. He is the man of steel who saves people's lives and fights for truth and justice. Why do people invent these characters? What are their qualities? Do you enjoy stories or movies about superheroes? Why or why not?

4. Leaders such as Hitler in Germany or Stalin in Russia or Mao in China *seemed* to some people to be heroes at one time in history. Are they real heroes? Can heroes be dangerous? Why or why not?

5. Read the following paragraph about heroes by a student. Then write a paragraph explaining whether you agree or disagree with the author.

   A hero is somebody who saves lives, somebody who cares about everything and everybody, someone who helps in difficult situations, someone who dies for people and a country. Do we really need heroes? Yes, we do. The past shows us that the world needs people to look up to—people who would make others fight against dictators, or people who would prevent others from starting wars. Even today, we need people who can stop the killing of innocent victims all over the world. But no one wants to do it and thousands of people die. So maybe we are a generation that wants to live comfortable lives, people who want to be left alone with their bank accounts and don't want to hear about other people dying in wars. Maybe we have forgotten heroes, or maybe they don't exist any more.

6. Write about a hero from your country. Why is this person important to the nation?

7. Look up information about a famous American. You can use the library and/or the Internet. Write a paragraph about the person's contribution to the nation. In your opinion, is he or she a hero? Why or why not? You may select one of these names or choose one of your own.

George Washington	Jim Thorpe
Thomas Jefferson	Charles Lindburgh
Abraham Lincoln	Jonas Salk
Harriet Tubman	John F. Kennedy
Susan B. Anthony	Neil Armstrong
Booker T. Washington	Rosa Parks
Thomas A. Edison	Cesar Chavez
Margaret Sanger	

3 WEATHERING THE STORM

WRITING INSTRUCTIONS

In this unit you will practice:
- giving instructions

Editing focus:
- imperatives
- modals
- adverbs of frequency

I ▸ Fluency Practice: Listing

"I just lost my job and had to move to a less expensive neighborhood, but I am weathering the storm, doing the best I can."

Discuss with a partner what you think the idiom weathering the storm *means.*

Imagine that a terrible hurricane is coming to your town. You are in danger, and you must leave your house to go to the nearest public shelter for safety. List five things you would take with you in such an emergency. Discuss your list with a partner.

II Reading for Writing

A hurricane is a tropical storm in the Atlantic Ocean or Caribbean Sea with winds of more than 74 miles an hour, rough seas, and high water levels.[1] Today there are scientific instruments to follow the progress of a hurricane so that people can prepare for it.

HURRICANE EMERGENCY PROCEDURES

Instructions from the United States Federal Emergency Management Agency

HURRICANE WATCH

The storm is 36 to 24 hours away.

- Turn on a battery-powered radio.
- Check emergency supplies.
- Put gas in the car.
- Bring in outdoor furniture.
- Tie down the furniture you can't bring inside.
- Tape your windows crisscross.[2]
- Nail wooden boards across the taped windows.
- Turn the refrigerator temperature to the coldest setting.
- Store clean water in the bathtub or in bottles.

HURRICANE WARNING

The storm is expected to arrive within 24 hours.

- Listen to the radio for instructions.
- Store valuables in a waterproof container in the highest place in the house.
- Avoid elevators.
- Stay away from the windows.
- Keep a supply of flashlights and batteries.
- If electricity is lost, turn off all appliances.

EVACUATION ORDER

For severe storms, evacuate the area. Your life is nothing to play with. The police will show you the way to safe buildings inland, away from the storm.

When you hear the evacuation order:

- Unplug all appliances.
- Shut off the electricity.
- Turn off the main water valve.
- If possible, tell someone outside the storm area where you are going.
- Take your emergency supplies and warm clothing.
- Lock up your home and leave.

---

[1]In the Pacific Ocean or the China Sea, a tropical storm with winds of more than 74 miles per hour is called a typhoon.
[2]*crisscross:* in an X shape

A. General Understanding

Mark the stages of hurricane preparation in order.

_____ evacuation

_____ watch

_____ warning

With a partner, read the instructions and put a check (✓) in the appropriate column. You may put a check in more than one column.

Instructions	Hurricane Watch	Hurricane Warning	Hurricane Evacuation
1. Stay away from windows.		✓	
2. Prepare the car.			
3. Take emergency supplies.			
4. Listen to the radio.			
5. Board up windows.			
6. Store water.			
7. Get out.			
8. Put valuable things away.			
9. Turn off electricity and water.			
10. Clear the yard.			

B. Words and Ideas

Letter to an Insurance Company

Use these words to fill in the blanks in the letter. Compare your answers with a partner's.

appliances	evacuate	flooded	shelter
store	unplug	waterproof	

Downstate Mutual Insurance Company
414 Main Street
Miami, Florida 33000

Dear Sirs,

We are writing to give you the information you need to settle the insurance claim on our house and its contents after the recent hurricane (policy number 43687J).

When the hurricane finally hit our area, conditions became very bad in a matter of hours. We had to _____ immediately. We
₁

went to an emergency _____ after doing what we could
₂

to protect our home. We had time to _____ our family
₃

papers in _____ containers before we left. When we
₄

came back, we found a lot of damage. The ground floor was completely

_____. Although we were careful to _____
₅   ₆

all the electrical _____, it took a long time to get the
₇

electricity back on because the wires were wet. There was a lot of

damage to our freezer and furniture.

We enclose here pictures of our house and receipts for the furniture and the food. We look forward to hearing from you soon.

Sincerely,

Ann Carter

Ann Carter

Note: In formal or business letters, you can use either a colon or a comma in the salutation. For informal letters, commas are normally used.

III Prewriting Activities

1. Giving and Explaining Instructions

Direct Commands

Use the imperative (base form of the verb):

Store　　water in the bathtub.

BASE FORM

Advice and Obligation

Use the modal *should* + base form of the verb:

You　　**should**　　**store**　　water in the bathtub.

　　　　SHOULD　　BASE FORM

Write instructions and explanations to answer these questions. You can use the reading to help you. Share your answers with a partner.

1. How can you save water?

   Store water in the bathtub.

   Why?

   You should store water in the bathtub for drinking and washing because the water system may break down.

2. How do you protect yourself from broken glass?

   _____

   Why?

   _____

   _____

3. What do you do with your furniture?

   _____

   Why?

   _____

   _____

4. How do you prepare your car for evacuation?

_____

Why?

_____

_____

5. How do you find out about an evacuation order?

_____

Why?

_____

_____

2. Open for Discussion

Discuss these questions in a small group.

1. Do you live in a place where natural disasters occur? Are there hurricanes? snow storms? earthquakes? floods? tornadoes? volcanoes?

2. Have you ever experienced an emergency situation? Where were you and what happened? Was it a natural disaster or a man-made disaster? Were you alone? Were you afraid? How did you overcome your fear?

3. When you see television news programs or movies about disasters, what do you think? How do you feel?

IV Structured Writing Focus

YOUR TASK

Write a list of instructions for a topic of your choice. For example, you could write about how to create a Web site on the Internet or how to find a job. Then put the instructions in paragraph form with an explanation for each instruction.

ALTERNATIVE TASK: Give advice on being a good friend (or boyfriend/girlfriend). List your ideas. Then put them in paragraph form with an explanation for each piece of advice.

Giving Instructions or Advice

From List to Paragraph

Read this list of instructions.

GOING HOME AFTER A HURRICANE

- Be careful when you enter the house.
- Open all the windows and doors.
- Check for gas leaks, electrical system damage, and water damage.
- Take pictures of the damage to the house and its contents.
- Start cleaning your house.

To turn the list into a paragraph, you need to add some transition words to connect one sentence to another:

first	then	next	also	in addition	finally

Read this paragraph. Circle all the transition words. Then underline the reasons and explanations. Put a check (✓) in front of the topic sentence and the concluding sentence.

GOING HOME AFTER A HURRICANE

When the storm is over, it is natural to want to go home as soon as possible. When it is safe to return, you should take the following steps: First, be careful when you enter your house. There may be snakes or other animals that the flood washed in. Then, open all the windows and doors. You should let the fresh air dry the house. Next, check for gas leaks, electrical system damage, and water damage. Any of these problems can be very dangerous. If you find anything wrong, you should turn off the power and call the gas company, the electric company, or the water company for help. In addition, take pictures of the damage to the house and its contents. You will need this proof for the insurance company. Finally, start cleaning your house. This is the hardest job because you must pick up the pieces of your life and put it back together. When you return to your house after a hurricane, be patient! It takes a long time to return to normal.

A. Starting to Write

1. Brainstorming

Before you write your list of instructions or advice, think about these questions:

How to _____
(your topic)

- Why is it important to know how to do this?
- What are the steps in the process?
- What dangers are there if you don't do it right?
- Can anyone do this? Is it easy or difficult to do it?

Now make some notes. You do not have to write complete sentences or worry about grammar.

General ideas (for the task of your choice)

_____

_____

_____

_____

_____

_____

_____

_____

_____

_____

_____

_____

_____

_____

_____

_____

2. Organizing Your Notes

You can now begin to organize your first draft. First, use your notes to write a list of instructions on the left side of the chart. Then on the right side, write an explanation of each instruction in note form.

How to _____	Why?
_____	_____
_____	_____
_____	_____
_____	_____
_____	_____
_____	_____
_____	_____
_____	_____
_____	_____
_____	_____
_____	_____
_____	_____
_____	_____
_____	_____
_____	_____
_____	_____
_____	_____
_____	_____
_____	_____

B. Preparing the First Draft

*Look back at your notes. Write a **first draft** of your paragraph. This time write complete sentences. Try to use some of the structures and vocabulary you have practiced in this unit.*

Topic Sentence _____

_____

_____

Body _____

_____

_____

_____

_____

_____

_____

_____

_____

_____

_____

Concluding Sentence _____

_____

_____

C. Revising the First Draft

Read your paragraph to a partner.

CHECKLIST FOR REVISING THE FIRST DRAFT

When you listen to a partner's paragraph and think about your own, keep these questions in mind:

1. Is the first sentence a good introduction to the topic?
2. Are the instructions and advice organized in a logical way?
3. Are the explanations clear?
4. Is the last sentence an interesting conclusion?

---

*Now write a **second draft** that includes all the additions and changes.*

D. Editing the Second Draft

After you have written a second draft, proofread your work to find any errors and correct them. These guidelines and exercises should help.

1. Review of Imperatives and Modals

Imperatives

base form of the verb

Take blankets.
Don't **forget** to turn off the electricity.

Modals

modal + base form of the verb

	Forms		Meanings
I	**must close**	all the windows.	necessity
You	**mustn't wait**	too long to leave.	
He	**should listen**	to the radio.	advice, obligation*
She	**shouldn't forget**	to warn neighbors.	
They	**can't see**	in the dark.	ability, possibility
They	**can take**	their pets.	

Ought to has the same meaning as *should*.
Example: He ought to listen to the radio.
Ought to is rarely used in the negative.

Make any corrections that are necessary in the following instructions. Check your answers with a partner.

Before loading the wash, you **must take~~n~~** these steps:

1. You **should studied** all care labels in the clothes.
2. You **should to empty** all pockets.
3. You **shouldn't mixed** dark colors with light colors.
4. You **must pouring** a capful of detergent in the washer.
5. You **can to use** fabric softener if you choose.
6. **Not to overload** the machine!

2. Some Adverbs of Frequency with Imperatives and Modals

Imperatives

adverb + base form of the verb

Always take money with you.
Never wait too long.

adverb at the end

Check the gas **often.**
      sometimes.
      frequently.
      every two hours.

Modals

modal + adverb + base form of the verb

You **should always board up** the windows.
You **should often check** with your neighbors.
You **must never forget** to turn off the water.
You **can sometimes take** your valuables with you.

With a partner, make any corrections that are necessary in the following sentences. Some sentences are correct as is.

HOW TO BE A GOOD HUSBAND

1. Every couple (always) should ᵛexperience an unselfish feeling of love.

2. Love always the woman you marry at least as much as you love yourself.

3. Always be her best friend.

4. You should share frequently your feelings with each other.

5. Be never afraid to open up to each other.

6. Never be dishonest about money.

7. Disagreements about money can destroy often a marriage.

8. Finally, criticize her mother never!

E. Preparing the Final Draft

Reread your second draft and correct any errors you find. Put a check (✓) in each space as you edit for the points below. Then write your corrected final version.

CHECKLIST FOR EDITING THE SECOND DRAFT

____ imperatives

____ modals

____ adverbs of frequency with imperatives and modals

Additional Writing Opportunities

Choose one of the following topics and write a paragraph.

1. Your boss needs to learn English. Give advice to him or her on how to be an effective language learner.

2. What is your favorite dish from your culture? Write instructions for a friend who is not from your culture explaining how to prepare and cook this dish.

3. Explain to a colleague how to be successful in the career you know best.

4. Who do you go to when you need advice? Whose advice do you value, and why?

5. "Many people will walk in and out of your life, but only true friends will leave footprints in your heart."—Eleanor Roosevelt

   What do you think this quote means? Do you agree or disagree? Explain your answer.

6. Choose one of the following natural disasters: earthquakes, floods, tornadoes, or volcanoes. Research your topic and write a paragraph explaining the causes of that disaster.

4 THE BABY JESSICA CASE

In this unit you will practice:

- expressing opinions
- putting reasons in logical order
- writing a formal letter

Editing focus:

- logical organizers
- subject-verb agreement
- present real conditionals

I Fluency Practice: Freewriting

What is a family? Is it a group of people related by blood? Can it be any group of people who love and help each other? Is it a husband, wife, and children? What if a man and woman are living together but not married? What if there are no children? Are adopted children part of the family? What about stepchildren from a partner's previous marriage?

Write for ten minutes about what you think a family is. Try to express yourself as well as you can. Don't worry about mistakes. Share your writing with a partner.

II Reading for Writing

This reading is based on a true story. Later in the unit you will find out what finally happened.

THE BABY JESSICA CASE

The Schmidt[1] family calls her Anna. The DeBoers[2] call her Jessica. She is two and a half years old, and the judges must decide who can keep her.

The Schmidts

Jessica's birth mother, Cara Clausen, gave up her baby girl at birth because she couldn't take care of her. When Cara gave birth to Jessica at age 29, she was not married, and she decided to give up the baby for adoption. The man she said was the father also signed the papers giving up the baby girl. But Cara knew that this boyfriend was not the real father of the baby. She lied on the adoption papers.

Some time later, Cara went back to Dan Schmidt, then 40 years old, who was Jessica's biological father. She decided that she wanted her baby back and she told Dan the truth. Dan already had two children by two different mothers (a boy and a girl, ages 17 and 12). He never wanted to give any support money to either child, and he never visited the girl. But Dan agreed to marry Cara and try to get their baby back.

Today, Cara's life has changed. She and Dan have gotten married and have another little girl who is five months old. Dan works as a truck driver. Cara Schmidt stays at home to take care of her child. The family lives in a small house in Blairsville, Iowa, a farming community. They think that blood ties are the most important thing for a family and a child.

The DeBoers

Roberta DeBoers and her husband, Jan, are the only parents Jessica has ever known. Roberta and Jan are both 35 years old. Jan is a printer and Roberta is an interior decorator. They have a successful life and live in a large house in the suburbs of Ann Arbor, Michigan. They were not able to have any children of their own, so two years ago they began the adoption procedure for this baby when she was a few months old. They called her Jessica. Jessica has a room of her own in their house and a playground in the backyard. Roberta DeBoers goes to work part-time and Jessica stays home with a baby-sitter while her mother works. Jessica calls Roberta "Mommy" and Jan "Daddy."

The DeBoers believe that Jessica is happy with them and that taking her away to strangers would hurt her very much. They feel they did the right thing when they accepted and loved this child that no one wanted.

---

[1] *Schmidt* is pronounced Sh-mit.
[2] *DeBoers* is pronounced D-beers.

Who should have Jessica? Some people think that the child should stay with the DeBoers where she is happy. Others feel that a biological family is the most important thing and that she should go with the Schmidts. What do you think?

A. General Understanding

Number these events in the correct order according to the story.

—— Cara gives up Jessica for adoption.

—— Cara and Dan have another little girl together.

—— Jessica goes to live with the DeBoers.

_1_ Jessica is born.

—— Cara and Dan get married.

—— The courts must decide who gets Jessica.

B. Words and Ideas

Two Families

Fill in the chart comparing the two families. You can go back to the reading to check on details. Discuss your answers with a partner.

Family Members	Age	Location	Job	Home
The Schmidts	Cara: 29 years old Dan: 40 years old			
The DeBoers				

Here are some statements comparing the two families:

Roberta DeBoer is older than Cara Schmidt.
Both Dan and Jan work hard.

Now write five new sentences comparing these two families.

1. _____

2. _____

3. _____

4. _____

5. _____

 # III Prewriting Activities

A. Opinions

1. How Do You Feel About This?

Answer these questions. Read your answers to a partner and discuss them.

1. Do you think adopted children should know they are adopted?

   • Most social workers today say that children <u>should know</u> the truth before they are one or two years old. You <u>shouldn't wait</u> until they are 18 or 20 because they will think their whole life was a lie.

   • I disagree with that. I think children <u>shouldn't know</u> that they are adopted until they grow up and can handle the truth. Maybe they <u>should never know</u>.*

   What do you think? _____

   _____

*Refer to Unit 3, "Weathering the Storm," page 41, for an explanation of the use of the modal *should*.

2. Should adopted children be able to find their biological parents? What if the biological parents have another family?

_____

_____

3. What if the biological family doesn't want any contact? If parents give up a child for adoption, should their privacy be respected?

_____

_____

4. What is the best way for parents to give a child a happy childhood?

_____

_____

5. What kind of people should become adoptive parents?

_____

_____

2. Whose Opinion Is It?

In a small group, discuss who might make the following statements, biological parents or adoptive parents. Put a check (✓) in the appropriate column.

Statement	Biological Parents	Adoptive Parents
1. All children want to know their natural parents.		
2. Giving birth doesn't make you a good parent.		
3. People will be afraid to adopt children if Jessica is given back to her natural parents.		
4. No one can love a child as much as the natural parents do.		
5. Your real parents are the ones who raised you.		
6. People should have four weeks to ask for a child back from adoption. After that time, they should lose their parental rights and the adoption should become final.		
7. "Blood is thicker than water." (a proverb)		

3. Opinion Letter

Use these words to fill in the blanks in the letter. Then complete the letter yourself.

adoptive parents	lied	birth parents
suburb	gave up	take care of

Dear Family,

    I am writing this letter to tell everyone what has happened to our Cara. She has decided to get back the baby she _____
1
for adoption. This was a shock to me—I didn't know anything about this. The baby is living with her _____ , the DeBoers, who live
2
in a _____ of Ann Arbor, Michigan. They seem to be good
3
people who support her and _____ her. How will the baby
4
feel if we take her away from the only family she has ever known?

    I'm not sure what to think. Our Cara has made some mistakes, as you know. She _____ to Dan and her other boyfriend
5
and to the adoption agency. But Dan and Cara are the baby's

_____ and they want her back.
6

    I think the family should _____

_____

_____

_____

_____

              Much love,

              Aunt Martha

B. Optional Prewriting Task

Write a paragraph on one of the following topics:

1. You are Cara Clausen. Explain why you changed your mind about the adoption. Give examples to prove that you are a more responsible person today.

2. You are Roberta or Jan DeBoer. Explain why you adopted Jessica and how much you love her. Tell how you feel about the problems with the Schmidt family.

IV Structured Writing Focus

> Write a letter to the editor of a newspaper telling why you think Baby Jessica should stay with the DeBoers, her adoptive parents, or go to the Schmidts, her birth parents.
>
> ALTERNATIVE TASK: Write a letter to the editor of a newspaper explaining what good parents should or shouldn't do when raising their children.

Opinion Letter to a Newspaper

Look at the format of the formal letter below. Read the letter and answer the questions that follow.

Your Address → 77 Ingram Street
Forest Hills, NY 11375

Date → June 1, 2001

Receiver's Address → The Editor
The New York Times
229 West 43rd Street
New York, NY 10036

Salutation → To the Editor:

Body of the Letter → In the May 4 edition of your newspaper, there was an interesting article about adoption, "To Adopt or Not to Adopt." I think adoption is a good idea for many reasons. First of all, adoption provides a family life for children with no parents. A second reason is that adoption gives couples who cannot have children the chance to become parents. In addition, adoption saves money for the government because it reduces the number of people the government has to take care of. Finally, adoption is good for our society because children raised in loving families become good citizens. This is why I am in favor of adoption.

Closing → Sincerely,

Signature → *Alex Tilitz*

Printed Name → Alex Tilitz

1. Does the writer agree or disagree with adoption?

2. Underline the main idea of the letter.

3. How many reasons does the writer give to support his opinion?

4. Circle the words that introduce each reason.

A. Starting to Write

Brainstorming

What is your personal opinion of the Baby Jessica case? Who should get Jessica? Should the case be decided on legal questions? moral questions? parents' rights? the best interests of the child?

To help you think further about the situation, complete each of the following sentences with three possible endings. Share your answers with a partner.

If Jessica remains with the DeBoers, _____

_____

_____

If Jessica goes to live with the Schmidts, _____

_____

_____

Write some notes for your letter. You do not need to write complete sentences or worry about grammar.

Your Opinion

_____

_____

_____

Reasons and Explanations

_____

_____

_____

_____

Concluding Sentence

_____

_____

B. Preparing the First Draft

After you have written your notes, think about what an opinion letter needs. The opinion letter about adoption on page 51 begins with a clear general statement: "Adoption is a good idea." Then the letter gives several reasons to support that opinion.

1. Giving Several Reasons

Look back at the letter and complete the outline of the reasons below.

"Adoption is a good idea."

1. family

    a. Children without parents can become part of a family.
    b. Couples with no children can become parents.

2. government

    The government saves money because _____

    _____

3. society as a whole

    _____

    _____

2. Putting Reasons in Logical Order

The reasons in the letter move from smaller to larger—from family to government to our society as a whole.

Here are some other ways to organize:

most important information	least important information
↓	↓
least important information	most important information

economic or political reasons	past	immediate effects
↓	↓	↓
personal reasons	present	long-term effects
	↓	
	future	

There are many possibilities. The way you organize your ideas is your decision, but you must be sure to support your opinion adequately and logically.

3. Practice with Opinions

Put a check (✓) next to the statements that express a clear opinion about adoption.

_____ a. I don't agree with adoption.

_____ b. Adoption is a good solution for some families, but not for every family.

_____ c. I am an adopted child.

_____ d. Maybe adoption is good, maybe adoption is bad.

Put a check (✓) next to the reasons that support the opinion "I disagree with adoption for several reasons."

_____ a. Adoption mixes family and strangers, and an adopted child can never really love an adopted family.

_____ b. A well-ordered society needs clear blood ties.

_____ c. Adoption is better if the child is under two years old.

_____ d. The family can never know the child's full medical history.

_____ e. Adoption is good for the government.

_____ f. A person who can't have children should accept nature's decision because it is dangerous to go against destiny.

_____ g. A family inheritance could be given away to outsiders.

Go back to the reasons above and write the letters of the ones you checked next to these three general categories:

the individual person: _____

the family: _____

society as a whole: _____

Complete the paragraph below by using some of these transition words to connect one sentence to another.

First of all,	**First,**
A second reason is that	**Second,**
In addition,	**Third,**
Also,	
Finally,	**Finally,**

I disagree with adoption for several reasons. **First of all,** a person who can't have children should just accept nature's decision because it is dangerous to go against destiny. **A second reason is that** adoption mixes family and strangers, and an adopted child can never really love an adoptive family. _____

_____

_____

_____

_____

_____

Finally, _____

_____

_____

For all these reasons, I think adoption is just not a good idea.

*Look back at your notes. Write a **first draft** of your letter. This time write complete sentences. Try to use some of the structures and vocabulary you have practiced in this unit.*

C. Revising the First Draft

Read your letter to a partner.

CHECKLIST FOR REVISING THE FIRST DRAFT

Revising means focusing on ideas and organization, not on grammar. When you listen to your partner's letter and discuss your own, keep these questions in mind:

1. Does the letter express a clear opinion?
2. Are several reasons given?
3. Are the reasons carefully explained?
4. How does the writer organize the reasons?

Commenting on Other Students' Writing

Read the three excerpts from letters to the editor* on the next page, and discuss them with a partner.

- Which letter do you like best?

- Which letter do you agree with?

- Are the ideas presented logically and clearly?

- Would you suggest any changes in the letters?

---

*Refer to page 51 for the full format of a formal letter.

LETTER ONE

To the Editor:

We should think about Jessica first. The next few years are very important in the development of her personality. We should keep her safe and give her the opportunity to grow up feeling stable and loved. The DeBoers have given Jessica a chance to have a family, but Jessica needs to know about her blood ties. She also has the right to know that her mother changed her first decision to give her away. Therefore, Jessica should go with the Schmidts, but the DeBoers should have the right to see her twice a week. In addition, Jessica should be able to make her own decision when she becomes 13 years old.

Fabrizio

LETTER TWO

To the Editor:

I think that Jessica should stay with the DeBoers because this family can give many opportunities to Jessica. First of all, Jan and Roberta have stable jobs and good characters. They can make Jessica a good woman. Of course, the Schmidts are the natural parents of Jessica, but they gave her up. The DeBoers accepted her. In addition, Mrs. Schmidt lied about the father. If the Schmidts have a hard time again, they might do something bad to Jessica. Finally, I think a "raising mind" is more important than a "birthing mind." That's why the DeBoers should raise Jessica.

MinHee

LETTER THREE

To the Editor:

Since I read this story, I can't sleep. So, I decided to write a letter. I believe that for every child, love is the most important thing. The Schmidts gave the baby up for adoption. I think that action was very selfish. I would never give up a baby. I can't believe in the Schmidt family's love anymore. Please think about the DeBoers. Even though they are Jessica's adoptive family, they love her very much without blood ties. I believe no one can grow up well without real love. We should think about Jessica's future happiness.

Ayako

After you have discussed your letter and the other letters with a partner, you may want to reorganize your ideas, omit some, or add new ones.

*Write a **second draft** of your letter that makes your opinion as clear and complete as possible.*

D. Editing the Second Draft

After you have written a second draft, proofread your work to find any errors and correct them. These guidelines and exercises should help.

1. Subject-Verb Agreement

Make sure that all nouns and verbs agree with each other. For example, we say *I see* instead of *I sees*, and *he reads* instead of *he read*.

Look at the underlined subjects and verbs. Put a check (✓) if they agree, or correct them if they don't agree.

1. <u>Adoption is</u> a very good idea.   ✓ _____

2. <u>Blood ties is</u> very important.   _____ Blood ties are _____

3. <u>The DeBoers</u> both <u>works</u>.   _____

4. <u>Baby Jessica have lived</u> with
    the DeBoers since she was born.   _____

5. <u>The Schmidts wants</u> to raise
    Jessica now.   _____

6. <u>Mrs. Schmidt loves</u> both her
    children.   _____

7. <u>A judge is going</u> to make an
    important decision about
    Jessica's future.   _____

8. <u>We knows</u> how important the
    decision will be.   _____

Edit these paragraphs from a composition about adopted children. Underline the errors in subject-verb agreement and correct them. There are seven more errors.

takes
It take a lot of courage for a mother to give up her child for adoption.

She doesn't do this because she lacks love for the child she carried in her

womb. She do this because she don't think she is capable of giving her

child everything a baby deserve. Giving her child up for adoption is truly

an act of love.

Unfortunately, many children who learn that they was adopted feel

unhappy and abandoned. Even though they may has wonderful adoptive

families, they cannot forget what their mothers did. They spend their lives

looking for their birth mothers. When they finally find them, they often

realizes that their true parents is the ones who raised them and taught

them to love life.

2. The Present Real Conditional

With a partner, study these sentences and answer the questions that follow.

If Jessica **stays** with the DeBoers, she **will live** a comfortable life.

If the judge **wants** Jessica to live with the Schmidts, she **will be** with her natural parents.

1. Put circles around the two parts of each sentence.

2. In the part of the sentence starting with *if*, what is the tense of the verb?

3. What is the tense of the verb in the other part?

To show that the present influences the future, follow this pattern:

if   +   present tense   future tense

If Jessica **stays** with the DeBoers, she **will live** a comfortable life.

The verb in the "if" part of the sentence is always in the present tense. The verb in the other part, which shows the result, is in the future tense.

Note that the sentence can also be written with the result part first. In that case, there is no comma.

future tense   *if* + present tense

Jessica **will live** a comfortable life **if** she **stays** with the DeBoers.

Put the verbs in parentheses in the correct tense. Compare your answers with a partner's.

1. Cara Schmidt will have a second chance to show her love for Jessica

   if the judge _____ *(send)* Jessica to her.

2. If Jessica _____ *(live)* with the Schmidts, she

   _____ *(get)* to know a baby sister.

3. Jan and Roberta DeBoers _____ *(be)* very sad

   if they _____ *(lose)* Jessica.

4. If Jessica _____ *(change)* families at this young age,

   it is possible that she _____ *(experience)* psychological

   problems.

5. If Jessica is taken away from the DeBoers, other people

   _____ *(not want)* to adopt babies.

E. Preparing the Final Draft

Reread your second draft and correct any errors you find. Put a check (✓) in each space as you edit for the points below. Then write your corrected final version.

> **CHECKLIST FOR EDITING THE SECOND DRAFT**
>
> _____ subject–verb agreement
>
> _____ correct verb tenses in the present real conditional

Additional Writing Opportunities

Update: When Baby Jessica was almost three years old, the courts of the state of Michigan* ruled that she should live with Dan and Cara Schmidt, her biological parents. This was mainly because Dan Schmidt had never legally given up his daughter for adoption. He had never signed the papers because Cara said that another man was the father. Jessica is now called Anna Schmidt. She seems to have adjusted to her new life with the Schmidts. She calls Dan "Daddy" and Cara "Mommy." But she refers to Roberta DeBoer as "the other Mommy with the tail." (Roberta wears her hair in a ponytail.) More than a year after this decision, the DeBoers brought home a baby boy whom they hoped to adopt.

Choose one of the following topics:

1. Write a letter to the judges in the Baby Jessica case. Explain to them why you believe their decision was fair or unfair.

2. Write a letter to Jan and Roberta DeBoers. Explain to them why you believe they should adopt another child.

3. Write a letter to the United States Congress.** Explain why you think a special law should be passed to protect adoptive parents like Jan and Roberta DeBoers.

4. Write a letter to Dan and Cara Schmidt. Advise them on how to tell Anna her special story. If you don't think the Schmidts should tell their daughter the truth, explain to them why not.

5. Pretend that you are a birth parent who gave up a child for adoption many years ago. You are writing a letter to your child explaining why you gave up him or her for adoption. Explain to the child why you do or do not want to meet and get to know each other.

6. What is your definition of *family*? Write a paragraph explaining what a family is to you.

---

*The Supreme Court is the highest court in the country. It decides if laws agree with the U.S. Constitution or not, and it can overturn the decisions of all other courts. The Supreme Court was not asked to consider this case because the DeBoers did not want to cause Jessica any more suffering.
**Congress (the Senate and the House of Representatives) is the legislative branch of the U.S. government in Washington D.C. Congress makes the laws.

THE GREATEST INVENTION OF THE 20TH CENTURY

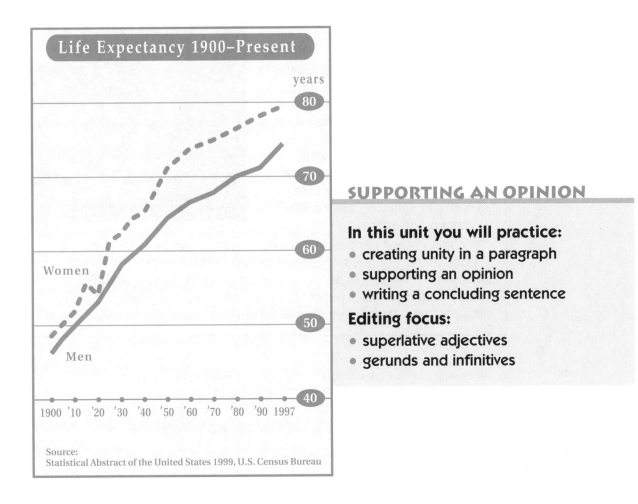

Life Expectancy 1900–Present

years

80

70

60

Women

50

Men

40

1900 '10 '20 '30 '40 '50 '60 '70 '80 '90 1997

Source:
Statistical Abstract of the United States 1999, U.S. Census Bureau

SUPPORTING AN OPINION

In this unit you will practice:
- creating unity in a paragraph
- supporting an opinion
- writing a concluding sentence

Editing focus:
- superlative adjectives
- gerunds and infinitives

I ◆ Fluency Practice: Listing Reasons

Why do you think people live longer today than they did in the past?

List as many reasons as you can to explain this fact. Write for five minutes. Share your list with a partner. Which reason do you think is the most important?

II ▸ Reading for Writing

Umberto Eco is a professor at the University of Bologna in Italy. He is also the author of *The Name of the Rose*, a very popular mystery novel set in 14th-century Europe. The following reading is part of an article Eco wrote for *The New York Times Magazine*.

In 1918, at the age of 40, my maternal grandfather[1] was stricken by[2] a form of influenza popularly known as the Spanish flu, which was decimating[3] much of Europe. Within a week, despite the efforts of three physicians,[4] he died. In 1972, at the age of 40, I was stricken by a serious illness that seemed similar to *la spagnola*.[5] Thanks to penicillin, after a week, I was up and about.

So it is easy to understand why, forgetting about atomic energy, space travel, and the computer, I persist in thinking that the most important invention of our time is penicillin (and, more generally, all those drugs that allow people today to reach the age of 80, while in the past they might have died at 50 or 60).

---

[1]*maternal grandfather:* grandfather on the mother's side; the mother's father
[2]*was stricken by* (strike, struck, stricken): was sick with
[3]*decimating:* killing approximately one in ten people
[4]*physicians:* medical doctors
[5]*"la spagnola":* Spanish flu; a strong influenza virus that brought fever, weakness, and death

A. General Understanding

Fill in the chart with information from the reading.

Date	Person	Illness	End Result
1918	Eco's grandfather		
1972			

With a partner, mark these statements true (T) or false (F) based on information in the reading.

_____ 1. Umberto Eco's grandfather received no medical attention.

_____ 2. The author is 40 years old.

_____ 3. Eco was cured in a week.

_____ 4. According to the author, antibiotics are more important than walking on the moon.

B. Words and Ideas

1. Open for Discussion

Discuss these questions in a small group.

1. Do you think that antibiotics are more important than walking on the moon? Why or why not?

2. If you were an inventor, what inventions would you create to help people enjoy a better life?

3. People can live longer today. Is this a good thing for our society? Does this cause any problems?

4. At what age do you think people get "old"?

5. What kind of life do you want for yourself when you get old?

2. The Discovery of Penicillin

Match the words on the left with a synonym (a word with a similar meaning) in the column on the right.

<u>d</u> 1. despite   a. taking a certain time

_____ 2. instead of   b. therefore

_____ 3. so   c. due to

_____ 4. thanks to   d. in spite of

_____ 5. although   e. while

_____ 6. within (a time)   f. rather than

Use these words to fill in the blanks in the story.

despite   instead of   so   thanks to   although   within

Some of the greatest discoveries happen by accident, but it takes a brilliant person to be able to understand the meaning of the accident. Millions of lives have been saved _____ penicillin. This
₁ miracle drug was discovered in 1928 by a Scottish doctor and researcher named Alexander Fleming.

Fleming was a poor boy and needed a scholarship to be able to go to medical school. Luckily, he got one. _____ a few years,
₂ he became the best student in the school and decided to do research.

One day he was looking at an experiment with bacteria.[1] He had left the cover off by mistake and saw that a mold, or fungus, was growing. _____ throwing it away, he looked at it carefully. In the
₃ area around the mold, all the bacteria were gone. _____
₄ this little mold killed bacteria, it left human tissue alive!

However, penicillin still couldn't be useful. _____ the
₅ great discovery in 1928, no one knew how to manufacture large quantities of the mold. English and American researchers finally found a way to do it, _____ penicillin could be mass-produced for
₆ everyone after World War II. Fleming won the Nobel Prize in medicine in 1947. It takes a lifetime of preparation to see the miracle in a moment.

---

[1]*bacteria:* one-celled life forms that can cause disease. They can be seen only under a microscope.

III ▸ Prewriting Activities

Inventions

1. *What do all these inventions have in common?*

cars	skyscrapers	subways	typewriters
movies	refrigerators	elevators	sewing machines
telephones	electric lights	the telegraph	washing machines
the radio	photographs		

Which of the inventions, if any, are essential in your life, and why? Discuss your answer in a small group.

2. *Choose one of the following 20th-century inventions that you think is the most important. Explain your choice in a small group.*

atomic energy

computers

genetic engineering

the Internet

jet planes

space travel

television

IV ▸ Structured Writing Focus

> **Write a paragraph about what you think is the world's greatest invention.**
>
> ALTERNATIVE TASK: **What do you think is the best thing or the worst thing about living 80 years or more?**

When you write your paragraph, you should include:

• a good **topic sentence** to start out.

• at least **three reasons** for your choice or opinion.

• an interesting **concluding sentence**.

A. Starting to Write

Brainstorming

Write notes for your paragraph.

What invention did you choose?* _____

Alternative task:
What is the best or worst thing about living for a long time? _____

_____

An idea for a **topic sentence:** _____

_____

Some **reasons** to support your main idea: _____

_____

_____

_____

_____

_____

A possible **concluding sentence:** _____

_____

B. Preparing the First Draft

Support and Concluding Sentence: Creating Unity in a Paragraph

Before you write, organize your thoughts and notes.

1. Be sure you have enough reasons to support your opinion or choice.

2. Make sure the reasons you give are all related to the main idea.

3. Plan your concluding sentence so that the reader will understand what you are trying to prove.

*You can refer to the Prewriting Activities section on page 67 for some ideas.

Read this paragraph and cross out the sentences that do not relate to the main idea. Discuss your decisions with a partner.

The Greatest Invention in My Life

Movies may seem to be just amusement and entertainment, but to me, they are the best answer to the loneliness and boredom of my life. In movies I meet wonderful people and see places I would never be able to see. Books are good, too, but I'm often too tired to read. I have been transported all over the world and learned about people with different customs and lifestyles. Movies are also a time machine, taking us back into the past or even giving us a glimpse of the future. From ancient Egypt to *Star Wars*, movies are a trip through time. I think the *Star Wars* movies are great, but some of my friends don't agree. Another reason I like movies is that for a few hours in the dark, I can feel that everyone in the audience is on my side. They may be strangers, but we laugh and cry together. The worst thing is when people sit down right in front of me. Movies can be thrilling and scary or joyous and funny. They take us away from our sadness and problems.

concluding sentence:
I cannot imagine my life without movies.

Discuss these questions with a partner.

1. How many reasons are given to support the idea that movies are the greatest invention in the author's life?

2. What are those reasons?

3. How does the concluding sentence relate to the main idea of the paragraph?

PARAGRAPH UNITY

Sentences that don't relate to the main idea:	Why?
"Books are good, too, but I'm often too tired to read."	The paragraph is concerned with movies, and this sentence is about books. This sentence doesn't belong.
"I think the *Star Wars* movies are great, but some of my friends don't agree."	This sentence is about what other people think about particular movies. This sentence is too specific.
"The worst thing is when people sit down right in front of me."	This sentence is about sitting in a movie theater. It is not about movies as the greatest invention.

A CONCLUDING SENTENCE:

- is the last sentence in a paragraph.
- reminds the reader of the main idea the writer is trying to prove.
- is a general statement, not another detail or reason.
- should fit with the main idea expressed in the topic sentence.

Topic sentence:

"Movies may seem to be just amusement and entertainment, but to me, they are the best answer to the loneliness and boredom of my life."

Concluding sentence:

"I cannot imagine my life without movies."

With a partner, put a check (✓) next to the sentences that belong in a paragraph about the advantages of old age, and put an "X" next to the sentences that don't. Then write your own concluding sentence.

THE ADVANTAGES OF OLD AGE

_____ a. I hope I live a long time because living to a very old age can bring so many joys.

_____ b. Who would want to live to get weak and ugly?

_____ c. Grandchildren are the best part of growing old. That's what I am most looking forward to. I can't imagine what they'll look like!

_____ d. Helping out my children is another reason I want to stay around, because I would be sad to leave them all alone.

_____ e. I also enjoy seeing what each day brings. The news from the world and from my neighborhood is always interesting to me.

_____ f. But living to an old age is only good if you have some money. I would rather die younger than have to take money from my children.

_____ g. It's true that there are bad things about growing old, such as getting hurt or weak. But I think I would still want to live even if that happens.

_____ h. I think it's ridiculous that people are allowed to drive when they are past 80. They are a danger to everyone.

_____ i. Finally, I certainly want to outlive the people I dislike, especially my mean and jealous brother-in-law.

Concluding sentence:

_____

_____

*Look back at your brainstorming notes on page 68. Decide which of the ideas will help you reach your conclusion. Write a **first draft** of your paragraph. This time write complete sentences. Try to use some of the vocabulary and structures you have practiced in this unit.*

C. Revising the First Draft

Read your paragraph to a partner or a friend outside class.

CHECKLIST FOR REVISING THE FIRST DRAFT

When you listen to your partner's paragraph and think about your own, keep these questions in mind:

1. Do all your sentences belong in the paragraph?

2. Are there any sentences that can be omitted?

3. Can you think of some sentences to add in order to make your ideas clearer to the reader?

4. Does the concluding statement fit with the main idea you are trying to prove?

---

*Now write a **second draft** that includes all the additions and changes.*

D. Editing the Second Draft

After you have written your second draft, proofread your work to find any errors and correct them. These guidelines and exercises should help.

1. Superlative Forms of Adjectives

Use the superlative form of an adjective when you want to compare more than two things and say that one of these things is *the most* or *the least* or *the best* or *the worst* of them all.

1. a. one-syllable adjectives ending in two vowels + consonant

   the + adjective + *-est*

   For Eco, penicillin was **the greatest** invention.

   b. one-syllable adjectives ending in a single vowel + consonant

   the + double the final consonant + *-est*

   Penicillin was **the hottest** thing on the market.

2. two-syllable adjectives ending in *-y*

   the + adjective (change *y* to *i*) + *-est*

   For Eco, **the loveliest** thing about science is helping people.

3. most two-syllable adjectives; all adjectives of three syllables or more

   the + *most* + adjective

   For Eco, penicillin was **the most important** discovery.

4. irregular superlative forms

   good → *the best*

   bad → *the worst*

   For Eco, a computer was a good invention, but penicillin was **the best** invention of all.

5. possessive forms with the superlative

   possessive form + superlative adjective

   When you use a possessive form with the superlative, the possessive form replaces *the*.

   Fleming's greatest discovery was penicillin.

   His greatest discovery was penicillin.

6. one of the best (things)

   one of + superlative + plural noun

   One of the best things about old age is having more free time.

Read this composition about paper and printing. If the superlative forms in **bold** *print are correct, put a check (✓) above them. If they are not correct, cross them out and write the correct forms. There are five more errors. Compare your answers with a partner's.*

Paper and Printing

Before the invention of books, people wrote on stone and clay, on rolls of papyrus made from plants in Egypt, or on dried animal skins in the Middle Ages. But to make a book, a real book as we know it today, you need paper and printing.

Paper was perhaps ~~greatest tool~~ **the greatest tool** for communication until the computer was invented. **The most good evidence** indicates that paper was invented by the Chinese between the years 250 B.C.E. and 105 C.E. Historians studying Asia have found **the most convincing proof** that paper was soon used to print money. Paper money is **one of the most useful inventions** in history, and it greatly helped the development of trade and commerce in China.

People make **biggest mistake** when they think that printing is entirely a Western discovery. In fact, the first ideas about printing also came to us from China. The Chinese made **the most large contribution** to the printing press. It is said that in 11th-century China, a blacksmith named Pi Sheng invented **the bestest system** for printing with blocks. Did this discovery travel to the West? Did a European make the discovery again by himself? Historians are not sure of the answer. But we do know that Johannes Gutenberg, a goldsmith in the city of Strasbourg, created the first European printing press with movable type in Europe around the year 1450. Without these contributions to paper and printing, it would not have been possible to invent the book, **one of the highest achievement** of the last millennium.

2. Gerunds and Infinitives

Study the following sentences:

I	**want**	**to understand**	how penicillin works.
	VERB	+ INFINITIVE	

We	**enjoy**	**living**	longer because of penicillin.
	VERB	+ GERUND	

Some verbs are followed by infinitives. Others are followed by gerunds. There is no general rule that can tell you when to use these different forms. This chart lists verbs according to the forms they go with and the patterns they follow.

1. Verb + Infinitive

decide	learn
need	plan
promise	remember
want	would like

I **would like to learn** more about penicillin.

2. Verb + Object + Infinitive

encourage	help
teach	tell
want	

Eco **wants us to understand** the importance of penicillin.

3. Verb + Gerund

enjoy	finish
imagine	stop
have (no) trouble	have (no) difficulty

Fleming **had trouble making** penicillin for the market.

4. Expressions + Preposition + Gerund

be afraid of	be interested in
be responsible for	be worried about
persist in	succeed in

Researchers **have succeeded in saving** many lives.

5. Verbs that can go with *either* gerund or infinitive

begin	hate
like	start

I **like learning** about science.

I **like to learn** about science.

Can You Imagine?

Read this imaginary interview with Guglielmo Marconi, the Italian Nobel Prize winner who invented the radio. With a partner, choose the correct form of the verb from the choices in parentheses.

Interviewer: Thanks to you and your invention of the wireless telegraph, people today enjoy ____listening____ (to listen, listening) to the radio and _____ (to watch, watching) television. We have no difficulty _____ (to receive, receiving) messages and pictures from satellites orbiting in outer space. Did you ever imagine _____ (to become, becoming) such a great inventor when you were a child?

Marconi: I always wanted _____ (to do, doing) something special, and I guess I did. I invented the telegraph when I was only 20 years old.

Interviewer: We know you didn't go to school until you were 12 years old. You started _____ (to study, studying) at home with a tutor. Do you think your home schooling helped you _____ (to become, becoming) an inventor?

Marconi: Well, yes, in a way. I learned _____ (to work, working) by myself and _____ (to trust, trusting) my own judgment. I enjoyed _____ (to study, studying) one-on-one with my tutor. He encouraged me _____ (to question, questioning) him all the time. He taught me never to be afraid of _____ (to make, making) a mistake.

Continue the interview. Write the correct forms of the verbs in the blanks.
Check your answers with a partner.

Interviewer: When did you first start _____working_____ *(work)* on your invention of the wireless telegraph?
13

Marconi: In the late 1800s. The telegraph had already made long-distance communication possible as long as there were wires connecting the points. I became very interested in _____ *(communicate)* without wires in 1894,
14
when I read an article about Heinrich Hertz's work on electromagnetic waves.

Interviewer: How long did it take to succeed in

_____ *(do)*
15
what you planned

_____ *(do)*?
16

Marconi: I spent at least two years _____ *(work)* on the
17
project before I showed it to anyone. I needed

_____ *(get)* financial assistance. But my
18
countrymen had difficulty _____ *(understand)*
19
the importance of my research. So in 1895, I went to Great Britain, my mother's native country, to get financial help. The British promised _____ *(give)* me
20
the money because they, too, were involved in the same kind of research. In 1896, when I was able to send a message in Morse code over nine miles, I succeeded in

_____ *(prove)* to the world that wireless
21
telegraphy had a future.

Interviewer: Do you have any advice for the unknown inventors of tomorrow?

Marconi: Never stop _____ (dream)!
22

E. Preparing the Final Draft

Reread your second draft and correct any errors you find. Put a check (✓) in each space as you edit for the points below. Then write your corrected final version.

CHECKLIST FOR EDITING THE SECOND DRAFT

_____ superlative forms of adjectives

_____ correct use of gerunds and infinitives

Additional Writing Opportunities

Choose one of the following topics and write a paragraph.

1. What imaginary invention would really change your life for the better? An automatic homework machine? A personal flying carpet? Why?

2. What do you think was the worst invention of the 20th century? Explain your answer.

3. Can you look into the future and predict the best invention of the 21st century? Explain your prediction.

4. You are organizing a time capsule to be left sealed until the year 3000. Choose five or six things that you want to include in that capsule to show future humans about our life today. Explain your choices.

5. Do you agree with Umberto Eco that antibiotics are more important than going to the moon? Should scientists work to discover the secrets of the universe, or should they work to benefit mankind?

6. "When you sell a man a book, you don't sell him 12 ounces of paper and ink and glue; you sell him a whole new life."—Christopher Morley

   What does this quote mean? Are books important in your life? Is there a particular book that you remember with great enjoyment?

7. Choose a famous inventor, and read about his or her life and work. Then write a brief paragraph explaining what the inventor did and how he or she did it.

DESCRIBING A PLACE

In this unit you will practice:
- writing a description of a place
- choosing an introductory sentence
- writing analogies

Editing focus:
- *there is / there are*
- noun and adjective word forms
- verbs: *feel* and *look*

I Fluency Practice: Freewriting

"Home Sweet Home." Discuss the meaning of this expression with a partner. Is home a wonderful place? Why would some people want to leave home?

What does home *mean to you? Write for ten minutes on your definition of the word* home. *Try to express yourself as well as you can. Don't worry about mistakes. Share your writing with a partner.*

II ▶ Reading for Writing

In this reading from *The House on Mango Street*, by Sandra Cisneros, a young girl named Esperanza writes about her home.

The house on Mango Street is ours, and we don't have to pay rent to anybody, or share the yard with the people downstairs, or be careful not to make too much noise, and there isn't a landlord banging on the ceiling with a broom. But even so, it's not the house we'd thought we'd get.

We had to leave the flat[1] on Loomis quick. The water pipes broke and the landlord wouldn't fix them because the house was too old. We had to leave fast. We were using the washroom next door and carrying water over in empty milk gallons. That's why Mama and Papa looked for a house, and that's why we moved into the house on Mango Street, far away, on the other side of town.

They always told us that one day we would move into a house, a real house that would be ours for always so we wouldn't have to move each year. And our house would have running water and pipes that worked. And inside it would have real stairs, not hallway stairs, but stairs inside like the houses on TV. And we'd have a basement and at least three washrooms so when we took a bath we wouldn't have to tell everybody. Our house would be white with trees around it, a great big yard and grass growing without a fence. This was the house Papa talked about when he held a lottery ticket and this was the house Mother dreamed up in the stories she told us before we went to bed.

But the house on Mango Street is not the way they told it at all. It's small and red with tight steps in front and windows so small you'd think they were holding their breath. Bricks are crumbling[2] in places, and the front door is so swollen[3] you have to push hard to get in. There is no front yard, only four little elms[4] the city planted by the curb.[5] Out back is a small garage for the car we don't own yet and a small yard that looks smaller between the two buildings on either side. There are stairs in our house, but they're ordinary hallway stairs, and the house has only one washroom. Everybody has to share a bedroom—Mama and Papa, Carlos and Kiki, me and Nenny.

---

[1]*flat:* an apartment
[2]*crumbling:* falling apart
[3]*swollen:* thicker or wider than usual
[4]*elm:* a kind of tree
[5]*curb:* the part of a sidewalk closest to the edge of the street

A. General Understanding

Discuss these questions in a small group.

1. Was the house on Mango Street this family's dream house?

2. Was the author happy to live in the house on Mango Street? Why or why not?

3. How do you know that her mother and father never really expected to live in their dream house? When did they talk about this house?

4. Why did the parents talk about an ideal or perfect house if it was only a dream?

With a partner, decide if the following words and phrases describe the apartment on Loomis Street, the house on Mango Street, or the ideal house. Put a check (✓) in the appropriate column.

	Loomis Street	Mango Street	Ideal House
1. pay rent	✓		
2. basement			
3. inside stairs			
4. share a yard			
5. bricks crumbling			
6. big yard			
7. three washrooms			
8. everyone shares a bedroom			
9. one washroom			
10. grass and trees			
11. pipes broken			
12. landlord			
13. four little elms			
14. garage			

B. Words and Ideas

Read the following sayings. In your own words, write what you think they mean. Discuss your answers with a partner.

1. "Home is where the heart is."

_____

_____

2. "A house is not a home."

_____

_____

3. "A man's home is his castle."

_____

_____

4. "Anywhere I hang my hat is home."

_____

_____

5. "You can't go home again."

_____

_____

6. "There's no place like home."

_____

_____

Share some sayings from your own language and culture.

III ◆ Prewriting Activities

A. Describing Shapes and Designs

1. Using Prepositions

Look at the shapes in the box. Then fill in the blanks in the description below, using the prepositions on the right.

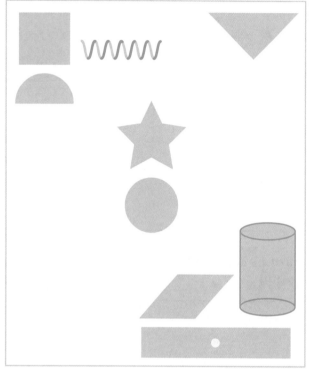

close to
near
next to

inside
outside

in the upper right-hand corner
lower left-hand corner

on the left
right

above / over
below / under

behind / in back of
in front of

In the middle of this arrangement of shapes we find a star with a circle _____1_____ it. In the upper left-hand corner there is a small square _____2_____ a semicircle. There is a horizontal spiral _____3_____ them. _____4_____ you will see an inverted triangle. On the bottom right, there is a cylinder that is very _____5_____ a parallelogram. _____6_____ the cylinder and the parallelogram, there is a rectangle with a dot _____7_____, in the center.

2. Your Design

Use the shapes from the drawing on page 83 to draw your own design. Then ask your partner to draw your design as you describe it to him or her. (Do not let your partner see your design before the task is finished.)

YOUR DESIGN

Listen to your partner's description. Draw the design as your partner describes it.

YOUR PARTNER'S DESIGN

Compare what you have drawn with your partner's original design. Are the pictures the same?

B. Describing a Room

Van Gogh's Room in Arles

Study this reproduction of van Gogh's Bedroom in Arles. *Write a one-paragraph description of what you see in this bedroom. Is this the room of a rich man? a poor man? What feeling does this room give you?*

C. Optional Prewriting Task

Examine the floor plan for this house in Nevada. The garage is very unusual! Do you like this house? Is it a good house for your needs or not? What kind of furniture would you choose for this house? Write a short paragraph explaining why you do or don't like this house.

IV Structured Writing Focus

YOUR TASK

Write a description of your room or your home. Make the reader understand your lifestyle, your choices, and what you think is important in the place where you live.

ALTERNATIVE TASK: In a magazine or book, find pictures of two rooms that have the same function (two bedrooms or two kitchens, for example) but look very different. Compare the two rooms. Make the reader understand what kind of person would live in each room and what lifestyle the room expresses.

When you describe your room, use the present tense and talk about:

• the **shape:** Is it a circle, rectangle, square?

• **materials** and **color:** What is the furniture made of? Wood? Plastic? Metal? What colors do you see? Red? Brown?

• the **placement** of furniture and objects: What things are *in front of*, *next to*, etc.?

• **feelings:** How does the room express your personality? This is the most important part of your writing.

A. Starting to Write

Brainstorming

Describe your room or your home. Draw a floor plan of it.

FLOOR PLAN

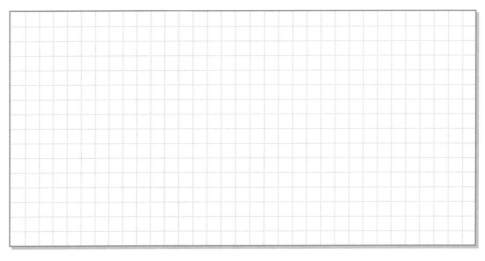

Write your description in note form. You do not have to write complete sentences or worry about grammar.

DESCRIPTION

Shape: _____

Materials: _____

Colors: _____

Placement of objects: _____

_____

_____

Feelings: _____

_____

_____

_____

_____

B. Preparing the First Draft

1. Introductory Sentences

A good introductory sentence will make your readers want to read your description. Begin with a sentence explaining why your room is special.

Not interesting:

I am going to describe my room.

This sentence tells us the topic (my room), but it is boring. There are no personal feelings or thoughts expressed.

More interesting:

My room is the only place where I can feel free.

This sentence makes us want to read on and learn more about the writer.

Read these sentences. Put a check (✓) next to the ones that are good first sentences, and discuss your answers with a partner.

_____ a. I would like to describe my room to you.

_____ b. My room is the one place where I feel free.

_____ c. My room is so messy!

_____ d. My home is my heaven, peaceful and calm.

_____ e. This is a description of my home.

_____ f. I don't care about furniture because all I need are books.

_____ g. Welcome to my room!

_____ h. Both these rooms are kitchens, but they would never please the same person.

_____ i. Here are two rooms that are very interesting.

Now write your first sentence here:

_____

_____

_____

2. Analogies

Your writing becomes more interesting when you use analogies. In an analogy you use the word *like* to say that one thing is like something else.

My house is like a shining star in the darkness of my life.

This is another way of saying that your house is the only place where you feel joy or happiness.

Discuss the meanings of these sentences with a partner.

1. This house is like a crumbling monument to the past.
2. My room is like an old shoe.
3. My house is like a sweet melody in a city of noise.
4. My house is like an American dream.

WRITING ANALOGIES

Write two analogies about your home or a room.

1. _____

2. _____

*Review your brainstorming notes. Write a **first draft** of your description. This time write complete sentences. Try to use some of the vocabulary and structures you have practiced in this unit. Don't forget to add an interesting concluding sentence.*

C. Revising the First Draft

Read your description to a partner.

CHECKLIST FOR REVISING THE FIRST DRAFT

When you listen to a partner's description and discuss your own, keep these questions in mind:

1. Is there a good introductory sentence?
2. Can you "see" the room or rooms that are being described?
3. Are the analogies effective?
4. Is there an interesting concluding sentence?

After discussion, you may decide to reword some sentences. You may want to include more information about how your room expresses your personality (or how the two rooms you have chosen express different lifestyles).

*Now write a **second draft** that includes all the additions and changes.*

D. Editing the Second Draft

After you have written the second draft, proofread your work to find any errors and correct them. These guidelines and exercises should help.

1. *There is / There are*

there is + singular noun

There is a lamp near the chair.

Use *there is* when the first noun in a series is singular.

On the table, **there is a vase**, some flowers, and a book.

there are + plural noun

There are many windows in the room.

Use *there are* when the first noun in a series is plural.

In the room, **there are chairs**, a table, and a bed.

A ROOM BY FRANK LLOYD WRIGHT

Look at this partial view of a room designed by the famous American architect Frank Lloyd Wright. The room is on display at the Metropolitan Museum of Art in New York City. Then read the analysis by a student on page 91, and fill in the blanks with there is *or* there are. *Compare your answers with a partner's.*

Name: Rosa Rodriguez
Course: Art and Architecture
Subject: A room designed by Frank Lloyd Wright*

A Visual Analysis of the Room

Frank Lloyd Wright was a famous American architect who believed in using simple designs and natural materials. This living room gives us a feeling of freedom and natural light because

_____there is_____ a lot of empty space in the middle and
1

_____ huge windows on two sides of the room.
2

_____ natural wood furniture along the walls and
3

natural wood floors. _____ a small desk by the
4

window, along with benches and chairs. _____ some
5

lamps with shades made of Japanese paper. On the right side of the

room _____ a fireplace made of reddish brown bricks.
6

_____ a European sculpture on one table and a
7

Buddhist statue on the other. They show a mixture of two cultures.

In the corner of the room, _____ a flower arrangement
8

of tree branches with red and yellow leaves. The wood all around

makes us feel warm and comfortable, while the earth colors, which

were so important to Frank Lloyd Wright, delight the eye.

---

*Frank Lloyd Wright (1867–1959) was an architect of the modern school. He called his style organic architecture, because he wanted houses to blend into their natural surroundings. He designed the Guggenheim Museum in New York City and many other structures in the United States and elsewhere, including Japan.

2. Noun and Adjective Word Forms

A **noun** is a person, place, thing, or idea.
You will like the **colors.**

An **adjective** describes or modifies a noun and tells us more about it.
You will like the **bright** and **cheerful** colors.

Some adjective endings are -*able*, -*ate*, -*ful*, and -*ious*.

Decide whether these words are nouns or adjectives.

	Noun	Adjective
taste	✓	
comfortable		✓
beautiful		
intimacy		
comfort		
color		
beauty		
intimate		
space		
colorful		
tasteful		
spacious		

Fill in the blanks in this paragraph with the correct adjective or noun form from the chart above. Compare your answers with a partner's.

Each person has a different idea of **b**<u>eauty</u>   . Rooms with a

lot of physical **s**   can be very attractive, but most of us

cannot afford such surroundings. We have to accept smaller, more

i   environments. Some of us use bright and cheerful

tones to make our rooms as **c**   as possible, but what

makes one person feel **c**   in a particular place may not

have the same effect on others. Some people like to have hundreds of books,

others like antique furniture, and still others prefer hi-tech computers and

entertainment centers. Indeed, **t**   is a very personal issue.

3. *Feel* and *Look* *

feel / look + adjective

This room **feels warm** and **beautiful.**

The wood floor **looks beautiful.**

gives a feeling of + noun

The room **gives** us **a feeling of warmth.**

Choose the word in parentheses that best completes each sentence in this paragraph. Compare your answers with a partner's.

Frank Lloyd Wright wanted his room to give us a feeling of

_____ (free, freedom) and _____ (airiness, airy).
1   2

Most ordinary rooms made him feel _____ (sadness, sad)
3

because they were too small and too crowded with objects. He believed

that empty space looked _____ (peace, peaceful) and
4

encouraged calm and tranquil feelings in people. His furniture always

looked _____ (neat, neatness) and _____
5   6

(cleanliness, clean). His use of wooden furniture and floors made people feel

close to nature and have a _____ (warm, warmth) feeling.
7

---

*Feel and look are verbs like be.
Correct: It feels bad. It looks bad. It is bad.
Incorrect: It feels badly. It looks badly. It is badly.

E. Preparing the Final Draft

Reread your second draft and correct any errors you find. Put a check (✓) in each space as you edit for the points below. Then write your corrected final version.

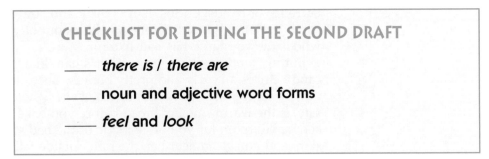

CHECKLIST FOR EDITING THE SECOND DRAFT

_____ **there is / there are**

_____ **noun and adjective word forms**

_____ **feel** and **look**

Additional Writing Opportunities

Choose one of the following topics and write a paragraph.

1. Find a picture of a house or a room that you like. Write a visual description and analysis of the picture. What kind of person do you think would live here? Would you like to live here? What feeling do you get from this place?

2. Compare a house of today with a house of the past. For example, during the Middle Ages in Europe, there was no privacy. Rich families lived with their servants. Poor families lived crowded together in small rooms. People had no separate areas of their own. How is this different from a modern house and the idea of privacy? You can use reference materials to research this question.

3. Describe a building in your country or city that you feel visitors should see in order to understand your culture or your idea of beauty.

4. Examine this reproduction of *Nighthawks* by Edward Hopper. Describe and analyze the picture. What is the painter trying to communicate about the place and the people?

5. Consider the use of analogies in the chapter called "Hairs," from *The House on Mango Street*. Then, using analogies, write a description of someone you know.

> Everybody in our family has different hair. My Papa's hair is like a broom, all up in the air. And me, my hair is lazy. It never obeys barrettes or bands. Carlos' hair is thick and straight. He doesn't need to comb it. Nenny's hair is slippery—slides out of your hand. And Kiki, who is the youngest, has hair like fur.
>
> But my mother's hair, my mother's hair, like little rosettes, like little candy circles all curly and pretty because she pinned it in pincurls all day, sweet to put your nose into when she is holding you and you feel safe, is the warm smell of bread before you bake it, is the smell when she makes room for you on her side of the bed still warm with her skin, and you sleep near her, the rain outside falling and Papa snoring. The snoring, the rain, and Mama's hair that smells like bread.

SOLVING A
CROSS-CULTURAL
BUSINESS PROBLEM

In this unit you will practice:
- writing a memo
- showing cause and effect

Editing focus:
- connectors:
  because, therefore
- infinitive of purpose
- verb tense logic

Fluency Practice: Freewriting

Have you ever been to an amusement park? Why do you think people like amusement parks so much? Do you like them? Have you ever been to an amusement park in another country?

Write for ten minutes about these questions. Share your writing with a partner.

II ▸ Reading for Writing

A MOUSE GOES TO PARIS

The Disney Company chose Paris for its European amusement park, Euro-Disney, because 17 million Europeans live less than a two-hour car ride from Paris. Another 310 million Europeans can fly to Paris in two hours or less. Also, the French government offered to contribute a large sum of money to this $5 billion project. In exchange, Disney agreed to create 30,000 new jobs for French people and share the profits with France. Today, Euro-Disney is called Disneyland Paris. It is a healthy, profit-making company; however, at the beginning, there were several problems.

Notes on a Paris Theme Park

Disney Company's Decisions	French Culture and Expectations
1. no alcohol allowed	a glass of wine for lunch is usual
2. Europeans were given breakfasts of coffee and croissants	most Europeans wanted "American breakfasts" of bacon and eggs
3. lunch was planned from 11:00 to 1:00	everyone wanted to eat at the usual time: 12:30
4. lunches cost $10–$15	too expensive for fast food
5. set up American-style rules for workers: always smile, obey your supervisor, no smoking, no earrings, no beards	rules were too rigid—most workers were students (10% left in first 9 weeks)
6. built many Disney hotels in the suburb where the park was located	most people chose Paris hotels; very few stayed in Disney hotels—too many empty hotel rooms
7. thought Friday would be the busiest day—hired extra workers for Friday	busiest day was Monday—not enough workers hired for Monday
8. thought everyone would take their children and not listen to intellectuals	some intellectuals condemned the park as "American imperialism" and told people not to go—many didn't go

A. General Understanding

Mark these statements true (T) or false (F). Check your answers with a partner.

_____ 1. The French government did not want the Disney Company to build an amusement park in Paris.

_____ 2. Three hundred twenty-seven million Europeans can get to Euro-Disney in two hours or less.

_____ 3. The Disney Company fully adapted to French ways.

Complete these sentences based on information in the reading. Use your own words. Compare your answers with a partner's.

1. The Disney Company served a breakfast of coffee and croissants, but

   _____

2. Disney thought the busiest day would be Friday; however, _____

   _____

3. Many French people wanted to drink wine with their lunches, but

   _____

4. The Disney Company thought most customers wanted to stay at

   Disney hotels; however, _____

   _____

Write two sentences of your own about Euro-Disney, using but *and* however. *You can use the reading to help you.*

5. _____

   _____

6. _____

   _____

Note: In sentences that use contrasting conjunctions, put a semicolon or a period before *however* and a comma after *however*. Put a comma before *but* when *but* joins two sentences.

- The Disney Company thought most people would eat between 11:00 and 2:00**; however,** most customers wanted to eat at 12:30.
- The Disney Company thought most people would eat between 11:00 and 2:00**. However,** most customers wanted to eat at 12:30.
- The Disney Company thought most people would eat between 11:00 and 2:00**, but** most customers wanted to eat at 12:30.

B. Words and Ideas

1. Open for Discussion

Discuss these questions in a small group.

1. What food or drink is typical of your culture or of where you live now? What does it taste like? How do you make it?

2. Do you like eating food from other countries? Which food in particular?

3. Do you like eating in American fast-food restaurants? Why or why not?

4. Have you ever been to an American fast-food restaurant in another country? Are the restaurants exactly the same as in the United States?

5. Do Americans like to eat food from your culture? Do they change the food a little, a lot, or not at all?

2. Reading Between the Lines

Discuss these questions with a partner and then write the answers. You won't find the answers stated directly in the reading. You will have to "read between the lines." You can check your answers in the back of the book.

1. Why do you think Disney did not put its European theme park in Norway or Italy? (*Hint:* Look at a map.)

   _____

   _____

   _____

2. Why did the French government offer a lot of money and land to Disney to encourage the company to come to France?

   _____

   _____

   _____

3. Why do you think some French intellectuals dislike American culture?

   _____

   _____

   _____

4. Why do you think Disney decided to build a new amusement park in Hong Kong?

_____

_____

_____

III ◆ Prewriting Activities

Business Practices Around the World

1. Our Poll

First, answer these questions, based on what you know about your culture. Then write the answers you think most American business people would give. Discuss your answers in a small group.

	In Your Culture	In U.S. Business Culture
1. If a meeting were called for 9 A.M., what time would people arrive? **a.** 8:58　　**b.** 9:00　　**c.** 9:15		
2. Do you call a business associate by his or her title? last name? first name? **a.** title　　**b.** last name　　**c.** first name		
3. Do you interrupt a speaker if you don't understand what he or she is saying? **a.** yes　　**b.** no　　**c.** not if he or she is the boss		
4. Is it acceptable to use humor during a meeting? **a.** yes　　**b.** no　　**c.** only if you're the CEO[1]		
5. How close do you stand while talking to someone? **a.** 1 foot away　　**b.** 2 feet away　　**c.** 3 feet away		

_____

[1]*CEO:* chief executive officer, the head of the company

2. Cultural Misunderstandings

Fill in the information about Euro-Disney problems in each category. Then write a sentence about what people from your culture would think about these problems (or what you personally think). Compare your answers in a small group.

Category	Euro-Disney Problems	How would people from your culture react? Would you feel the same way?
Schedules	Euro-Disney planners thought Friday would be the busiest day, not Monday.	
Food		
Hotels		
Work Rules		
Attitude Toward U.S. Culture		

IV Structured Writing Focus

Write a two-paragraph memo suggesting a solution to one of the problems at Euro-Disney: food, hotels, schedules, or work rules.

ALTERNATIVE TASK: **Write a memo suggesting a solution to another business problem of your choice.**

A memo is an interoffice letter. It is written from one employee to another employee in the same company. A memo must be short and clear.

Read this imaginary memo about a fictitious problem with the French train service, and with a partner, discuss the questions that follow.

MEMO

To: CEO, Euro-Disney, Paris
From: Dan Smith, Transportation Manager
Re: Trains to Euro-Disney
Date: November 5, 1993

Positive beginning

The problem

We are all very glad that the new train line has opened to take people to Euro-Disney just outside Paris. However, I must report that the trains are very crowded and uncomfortable. This is especially true at the busiest times when many people are trying to get to work. We are losing money because the trip from Paris is so disagreeable.

Suggested solutions

Benefits to the company

In order to attract more visitors to the park, we must ask the government to put more trains in service during peak hours. There are also many tourists who do not speak French; therefore, we need train employees who speak English and other languages at the information desks in train stations. If we do this, I'm sure more visitors will come to Euro-Disney in comfort and safety.

1. Who wrote the memo? Who was the memo sent to?
2. Can you tell what the memo is about before you read it? How?
3. What is the problem for Euro-Disney?
4. What solutions does the employee suggest? Are they good solutions?

A. Starting to Write

Brainstorming

Make some notes for your memo to the Disney Company or to the company of your choice. You can add some details from your imagination. You don't have to write complete sentences or worry about grammar.

A positive beginning about the company	_____ _____ _____
The problem	_____ _____ _____
Suggested solutions	_____ _____ _____
Effects of the solutions and benefits to the company	_____ _____ _____

B. Preparing the First Draft

1. Using Connectors to Show Cause and Effect

Use *because* to show the cause of a problem.

People feel very crowded **because** there are not enough trains.

Use *therefore* to show the effect or result of a problem. *Therefore* has the same meaning as *so*. *Therefore* is more formal.*

The trains are very crowded; **therefore**, people are not coming to Euro-Disney.

---

*Therefore can also begin a sentence. It can have a period before the word and a comma after the word. There is no change in meaning.
Example: The trains are very crowded. **Therefore**, people are not coming to Euro-Disney.

Fill in the blanks with because *or* therefore, *and put in punctuation if necessary. Compare your answers with a partner's.*

1. The trains to Euro-Disney are very crowded _____ more trains should be put in service during peak hours.

2. Some people hesitate to plan a trip to the Euro-Disney theme park _____ they don't speak French.

3. There will be additional trains going to the Euro-Disney station _____ people will feel more comfortable traveling there by train.

Combine these sentences to make one sentence using because *or* therefore. *Compare your sentences with a partner's.*

4. There will be more people speaking English, Spanish, Italian, and German at train stations on the line to Euro-Disney. More tourists will be able to find their way around.

   _____

   _____

5. Euro-Disney expects more people to come to their theme park. They are making travel arrangements easier.

   _____

   _____

2. Cause and Effect in Your Memo

Using because *and* therefore, *write one sentence showing the cause of the problem you are going to write about in your memo and one sentence about the effects of a solution you are proposing.*

1. Cause *(because)*:

   _____

   _____

2. Effect *(therefore)*:

   _____

   _____

3. Using the Appropriate Tone

When you write for business, you must use impersonal language; this is not a letter to a friend. You must also avoid presenting your ideas in an aggressive way.

Read these sentences. With a partner, put a check (✓) next to the statements that are acceptable for business use. Put an "X" next to the statements that are not appropriate. Check your answers in the back of the book.

_____ a. We look forward to hearing your reaction as soon as possible.

_____ b. Only an idiot would make such a stupid decision.

_____ c. Please consider our request.

_____ d. I would appreciate your cooperation because I am so sick and tired of dealing with this problem myself.

_____ e. If you don't do what we suggest, you can just get out of the company right now.

_____ f. If you accept this proposal, you will see that the future of the company will be much better.

_____ g. We believe these proposals will help the company move in a positive direction.

*You are now ready to write a **first draft** of your memo. Look back at your notes. This time write complete sentences. Try to use some of the structures and vocabulary you have practiced in this unit.*

C. Revising the First Draft

Read your memo to a partner.

CHECKLIST FOR REVISING THE FIRST DRAFT

When you listen to your partner's memo and discuss your own, keep these questions in mind:

1. Does the memo start on a positive note?
2. Is the problem clearly explained?
3. Is the cause of the problem given?
4. Is the suggested solution clear?
5. What are the effects of the solution?
6. Is the tone of the memo appropriate?

---

*Now write a **second draft** of your memo that makes the problem and your solution as clear as possible.*

D. Editing the Second Draft

After you have written a second draft, proofread your work to find any errors and correct them. These guidelines and exercises should help.

1. Infinitive of Purpose

Use an infinitive to explain the purpose of an action.

infinitive: *to* + base form of the verb

We should add new trains **to make** our passengers more comfortable.

You can also use the longer form to explain a purpose.

in order + infinitive

We should add new trains **in order to make** our passengers more comfortable.

Answer each of the following questions with a complete sentence using an infinitive of purpose. Then share your ideas with a partner.

1. Why do you think Disney's work rules are so strict?

_____

_____

2. Why do you think Euro-Disney served French customers croissants and coffee for breakfast?

_____

_____

3. Why should business people study other cultures?

_____

_____

4. Why are you working so hard to learn English well?

_____

_____

2. Verb Tense Logic

GENERAL REMINDERS

now
Present tense: Euro-Disney **makes** money today.

in the past
Past tense: Euro-Disney **lost** money when it first opened in the 1990s.

in the future
Future tense: Many people **will enjoy** Euro-Disney in the years to come.

*Read the article on the next page about a new Disneyland planned for Hong Kong. If the verbs in **bold** print are in the correct tense, put a check (✓) above them. If the verbs are not in the correct tense, cross them out and write the correct tense. There are five more errors. Compare your answers with a partner's.*

In 1999 the Walt Disney Company and the Hong Kong government **agreed** ✔

to build a new theme park in the Hong Kong district of Penny Bay. They hope it

will be
~~**was**~~ ready to open in about six years. Discussions were long and difficult. It

takes both sides 13 months to come to an agreement.

Hong Kong Disneyland **will improve** Hong Kong's tourist industry. For

example, 1.4 million more tourists **came** to Hong Kong each year if the theme

park is built. In addition, there **will be** more jobs. Right now Hong Kong **had** a

high unemployment rate. This **will** surely **get** better.

Most Hong Kong residents **are** glad that the Disney characters **became**

official residents of Hong Kong. The Disney Company **was** happy to be close

to the huge Chinese market. The mood in Hong Kong and at Disney is one of

great expectations!

E. Preparing the Final Draft

Reread your second draft and correct any errors you find. Put a check (✓) in each space as you edit for the points below. Then write your corrected final version.

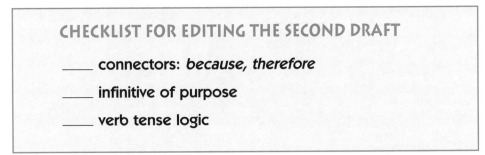

CHECKLIST FOR EDITING THE SECOND DRAFT

_____ **connectors:** *because, therefore*

_____ **infinitive of purpose**

_____ **verb tense logic**

Additional Writing Opportunities

Choose one of the following topics:

1. Visit some restaurants in your neighborhood. Choose one that has some problems with the food, the service, or the decor (the furniture and the atmosphere). Write a memo to the restaurant owner suggesting some necessary changes.

2. Have you ever lived for a while in another country? Give an example of a cultural misunderstanding that happened to you when you first arrived. Write about what occurred, why there was a problem, how the problem was resolved, and what you learned.

3. What kinds of fast-food restaurants do you like, if any? Explain your answer in a paragraph. Do you like fast food better than traditional cooking? Are these restaurants more convenient? Are they good for your health? Are these restaurants for young people or older people?

4. Write about the attitudes and behaviors people in your culture have toward business. Do you call people by their first names or family names? Do you use titles, such as Mr. Chairman? Is it important to arrive on time? How do men dress for business? How do women dress for business? Are women accepted in business? If you have experience in an American business, you can compare the attitudes and behaviors.

5. Walt Disney was a farm boy from the United States who became an art student and started an empire. Look up a biography of Disney in an encyclopedia or at the library. Write one or two paragraphs to tell your classmates about his life and work.

6. Write a review of a Disney movie, one you saw recently or one from your childhood. What was the movie about? Why did you like it or dislike it? Would you recommend this movie for a child?

8 The Crime That Didn't Happen

COMPARING NEWS STORIES

In this unit you will practice:

- comparing and contrasting
- making transitions and paragraph cohesion

Editing focus:

- articles
- nouns and determiners

 Fluency Practice: Freewriting

Many cities have problems with crime. Do you worry about crime? What do you do in your daily life to avoid becoming a crime victim? Do you think people should carry guns? Why do you think all this crime is happening?

Write for ten minutes about this topic. Try to express yourself as well as you can. Don't worry about mistakes. Share your writing with a partner.

10 Gs Can't Tempt Cabby

By AUSTIN PENNER
Daily News Staff Writer

NEW YORK — A tired cab driver was being called a hero today for his honesty. He returned $10,000 in cash that he found in the back of his taxi.

Taxi driver Syed Shah had just pulled into a gas station in New York City at 3 A.M. when he noticed a black purse on the floor. In the purse, he found $10,042, some credit cards, and a passport. Shah said, "I tried to find a telephone number or a beeper number, but I couldn't find anything." He had just finished a 12-hour work day. "I was tired, so I drove home and went to sleep."

Shah is 33 years old and came to the U.S. from Pakistan six years ago. He is a devout[1] Muslim, and he felt that it was his duty to return the money. So the next day, he drove to the Central Park police station and gave the money to the police. The police found the passenger.[2]

The lucky passenger was a woman from Belgium, Jacqueline Loreau, who was in New York visiting her sister. She said, "I'm very happy today. It was a real surprise. I didn't have any hope of getting it back. I know I shouldn't have put everything in that bag. I was going back to my sister's house, but I left it in the taxi." Ms. Loreau* called Shah "a good man" and promised to give him a reward.[3]

When asked why he returned the money, Shah said, "I am a religious person. I didn't want a burden on my head."

Violin Lost at Station

By BRANDON GOODMAN
New York Guardian

NEW YORK — Today a $100,000 violin was lost in Grand Central Station in New York City.

"I just put the violin down for a moment to make a telephone call," said John Coppola, a violinist with the Boston Symphony. "I know I shouldn't have left it standing there, but I only turned away for a moment. Then when I looked again, the violin was gone." Mr. Coppola was in New York for a visit with his family.

The police have searched the area and interviewed dozens of people, but no one noticed anyone carrying a violin.

Mr. Coppola has offered a big reward to anyone who brings back the violin. "Perhaps it was taken by mistake. If I get the violin back, I will pay a $5,000 reward and no questions asked." Such a beautiful instrument needs to be played by an artist. What will happen to it now? New Yorkers are hoping that someone gives it back because robberies like this give the city a bad name.

[1]*devout:* very religious, follows all teachings of a religion
[2]*passenger:* someone who rides in the back of the taxi and pays the driver
[3]*reward:* money given to thank people for their help
[4]*burden:* a load, a weight, a difficulty

*Note: **Mrs.** for a married woman or a woman of a certain age (pronounced "Misuz"); **Miss** for an unmarried woman; **Ms.**, the more modern form of address for women of any age, single or married (pronounced "Miz"); **Mr.** for men of any age, single or married (pronounced "Mister")

A. General Understanding

Comparing Two Stories

With a partner, fill in this chart comparing the story about the cabby with the story about the violin. What are the similarities? What are the differences?

Question	10 Gs Cabby	Lost Violin
Who lost something?	X Jacqueline Loreau X a tourist from Belgium ✓ not a New Yorker _____	John Coppola a visitor from Boston not a New Yorker _____
What was it?		
Where was it lost?		
How did it happen?		
Was the lost item found?		
Were the police involved? How?		
Was there a reward?		

Now go back and look at the information you have written in the chart. Put a check (✓) next to the facts that are similar. Put an "X" next to the facts that are different.

Complete these sentences comparing and contrasting the two news stories.
Then share your writing with a partner.

Similarities	Differences
both	*but/however*

1. Both John Coppola and Jacqueline Loreau _____

    _____

2. Ms. Loreau got her money back, but _____

    _____

3. The Belgian tourist lost $10,000 in cash; however, _____

    _____

4. In both stories _____

    _____

5. A reward was offered by _____

    _____

Now write your own sentences with similarities or differences.

6. _____

    _____

7. _____

    _____

8. _____

    _____

B. Words and Ideas

1. Open for Discussion

Discuss these questions in a small group.

1. Have you ever told a little lie, a "white lie"? If your friend put on some new clothes but didn't look good in them, would you tell your friend the truth?

2. Have you ever told a big lie? If so, what was the situation?

3. If you saw an old lady stealing a can of tuna fish from a store, what would you do?

4. If you saw someone cheating on a test, what would you do?

5. If you found $10,000, would you return it?

6. What do you think Mr. Shah meant when he said that he didn't want "a burden on his head"?

7. If Mr. Shah had not returned the money, do you think it would have been a crime?

2. Proverbs

Proverbs are short sayings that comment on daily life or tell a universally accepted truth. There are many proverbs in every language.

With a partner, write the meaning of each of these sayings in your own words. Then write whether you agree or disagree with the proverb.

1. "Finders keepers, losers weepers." (American proverb)

Meaning _____

_____

Your opinion _____

_____

2. "Honesty is the best policy." (English proverb)

Meaning _____

_____

Your opinion _____

_____

3. "Flattery makes friends; truth makes enemies." (Spanish proverb)

Meaning _____

_____

Your opinion _____

_____

4. "A man is not honest simply because he never had a chance to steal." (Russian proverb)

Meaning _____

_____

Your opinion _____

_____

5. "A thief believes that everyone steals." (unknown origin)

Meaning _____

_____

Your opinion _____

_____

Add a proverb from another language or from English that might relate to the stories in this unit, and explain what it means.

_____

_____

_____

III Prewriting Activities

A. Reading Newspapers

1. Where Can You Find It?

A newspaper is an important source of information. To be a good newspaper reader, you must know where to look for the information you need.

Work with a partner. Study the list of sections in an American newspaper in the box. Then write the letter of the section where you would find information about the topics that follow.

a. **Arts & Entertainment**	f. **Classified Advertisements**
b. **Business**	g. **Science**
c. **Editorials**	h. **Sports**
d. **National**	i. **Weather**
e. **International**	

—— 1. show times of a new movie

—— 2. a world trade conference

—— 3. the weather in Cancun, Mexico

—— 4. the latest stock market prices

—— 5. job openings

—— 6. the opinions of the newspaper editors

—— 7. a new discovery in biology

—— 8. candidates in a presidential election

—— 9. first-place winners in hockey

—— 10. a United Nations decision

—— 11. reviews of TV programs

—— 12. used cars for sale

—— 13. women's basketball scores

—— 14. apartment rentals

2. Headlines and Articles

In newspaper headlines, articles *(a, an, the)*, possessive adjectives *(his, her, their)*, and forms of the verb *be* are usually left out. The present tense is almost always used.

With a partner, rewrite the headlines on the left in complete sentences. Then match the headlines with the first sentences of the articles on the right.

1. POLICE CATCH THIEF—BIG CHASE DOWNTOWN

_____

_____

       a. International trade experts will gather next week to discuss agricultural issues.

2. WOMAN SAVES CHILD FROM BURNING BUILDING—POLICE ARREST SUSPECT

_____

_____

       b. A high school student was saved by her devoted dog yesterday, after she fell through the ice on West Pond.

       c. The police arrested a couple who left their baby in a carriage outside a city restaurant while they were eating lunch on Monday.

3. TRADE CONFERENCE IN GENEVA

_____

_____

       d. A bank robber led police on a two-hour chase through downtown yesterday, before they arrested him on the steps of City Hall.

4. DOG RESCUES TEEN

_____

_____

       e. A young teacher risked her life to save a child from a fire on Main Street. An arson suspect has been arrested.

5. PARENTS INSIDE, BABY OUTSIDE

_____

_____

B. Optional Prewriting Task

Writing a News Article

Newspaper articles usually begin with a general sentence telling what happened. The rest of the article gives all the details, including the names of the individuals involved.

Write a short newspaper article about a crime that happened to you or to someone you know. The article is for a local newspaper or a school magazine. Begin with a general statement and then give the details. Use your imagination to complete the article if you can't recall the exact details. Remember to use the past tense in your article.

IV Structured Writing Focus

Write two paragraphs showing the similarities (comparing) and differences (contrasting) the two newspaper stories you read in this unit.

ALTERNATIVE TASK: **Choose two newspaper stories about the same kind of topic (crime, politics, the arts). Write two paragraphs showing how these stories are similar to, and different from, each other.**

A. Starting to Write

Brainstorming

Use the columns below to write notes about how the stories "10 Gs Can't Tempt Cabby" and "Violin Lost at Station" are similar to, and different from, each other.

Similarities	Differences

B. Preparing the First Draft

1. Organizing Your Writing

One way to organize a short comparison is to use two paragraphs.

> **First Paragraph:**
> Similarities

> **Second Paragraph:**
> Differences

2. Making Transitions and Creating Paragraph Cohesion

A paragraph has cohesion when each sentence flows logically into the next. You can use some of the structures below to make your paragraphs more cohesive.

First Paragraph:	You can begin the first paragraph with one of these kinds of sentences:
	There are several similarities in the stories, "10 Gs Can't Tempt Cabby" and "Violin Lost at Station."
	The two stories, "10 Gs Can't Tempt Cabby" and "Violin Lost at Station," are similar in several ways.
Second Paragraph:	You can begin the second paragraph with one of these kinds of transitional sentences:
	Despite the similarities, there are some important differences between these two stories.
	Despite the similarities, these two stories are very different.
	Transitional sentences show a change from one idea or topic to the next.

*Review your brainstorming notes and write your **first draft**. This time write complete sentences. Try to use some of the vocabulary and structures you have practiced in this unit.*

Paragraph 1 _____

Similarities _____

_____

_____

_____

_____

_____

_____

Paragraph 2 _____

Differences _____

_____

_____

_____

_____

_____

_____

C. Revising the First Draft

Read your paragraphs to a partner.

CHECKLIST FOR REVISING THE FIRST DRAFT

When you listen to your partner's paragraphs and think about your own, keep these questions in mind:

1. Is there a good beginning sentence in the first paragraph?
2. Are all the similarities discussed in the first paragraph?
3. Is there a transitional sentence at the start of the second paragraph?
4. Are all the differences explained in the second paragraph?

---

*Now write a **second draft** that includes all the additions and changes.*

D. Editing the Second Draft

After you have written the second draft, proofread your work to find any errors and correct them. These guidelines and exercises should help.

1. Articles

RECOGNIZING THE NEED FOR AN ARTICLE

*A/An** or *the*, the indefinite or the definite article, must appear before every singular count noun. An article does not have to appear before noncount nouns.

Look at the following nouns and write a/an *before those that must have an article. Compare your answers with a partner's.*

_____ gun	_____ verdict	_____ crimes
_____ knife	_____ man	_____ taxi drivers
_____ people	_____ judge	_____ justice
_____ law	_____ honesty	_____ lawyer

WHEN TO USE A/AN OR THE

Count Nouns

Singular

A/An comes before singular count nouns when they are first mentioned. After that, use *the*.

Police officers arrested **a homeless man** yesterday. They said **the man** was bothering shoppers at Belmont Mall.

Plural

Plural count nouns do not always need *the* when they are first mentioned. The second time they are mentioned, use *the*.

Detectives questioned the homeless man and realized that he needed medical care. **The detectives** called Belmont Hospital.

Noncount Nouns

Noncount nouns don't need *a/an* or *the* when they are first mentioned. The second time they are mentioned, use *the*.

The homeless man was thirsty and asked for **water. The water** was cold and refreshing.

---

*An is used when the word following the article begins with a vowel sound: *an apple, an egg, an inch, an oven, an umbrella.*
but: *a European, a universal truth, a hotel, a yellow dog*—These words don't begin with a vowel sound.

Read this story and decide whether you need a/an, the, or no article before the nouns. Fill in the blanks. If you do not need an article, put an "X" in the blank. Compare your answers with a partner's.

A Close Call

Danielle Collins thought she had been the victim of a crime, and she has an interesting story to tell.

One day Ms. Collins, _____ editor for a New York publishing
                        1

company, needed to call her husband on the way to work.

_____ editor found _____ telephone booth and went right to it.
    2   3

She doesn't remember everything that happened after she got to

_____ phone booth. She thinks she placed her bag on the shelf,
    4

opened _____ bag, and took _____ money out of her wallet.
           5   6

Then she put _____ money into the phone, dialed her number, and
                 7

spoke to her husband. When she got to work, she no longer had her

wallet! _____ young man had been waiting outside the telephone
            8

booth while she was on the phone. "Did _____ young man take my
                                            9

wallet?" she wondered. _____ colleagues said she would probably
                          10

never see it again.

MORE ON WHEN TO USE **THE**

The must appear before singular count nouns or noncount nouns that are one of a kind:

The policeman who had to arrest homeless people was sad.
The teenage boy who was arrested called his parents.
The water that the homeless man drank was refreshing.

The must appear before singular count nouns and noncount nouns that are followed by *of* and a noun or noun phrase:

Some people are against **the policy of arresting the homeless.**
The water of the Hudson Valley is now clean.

With a partner, finish reading "A Close Call," and fill in the blanks with either a/an or the. Compare your answers with a partner's.

A Close Call (continued)

_____ first thought that ran through Ms. Collins's mind was that
11

she had been robbed. Before she moved to New York City a year ago

from _____ small town in Montana, people warned her to be careful.
12

Now it seemed that _____ fears of her Montana friends and family
13

had come true.

Later that morning, Ms. Collins got a call from _____ man. He
14

identified himself as Mr. James Young and told her that he had found her

wallet on _____ floor of a telephone booth at 23rd Street. Her
15

name and work number were in the wallet. He also told her that he

would be in _____ neighborhood where she works at lunchtime.
16

Mr. Young asked her if he could come to her office to return _____
17

wallet to her. Ms. Collins was delighted and naturally said, "Yes!"

When _____ man gave her wallet back, he told her that her
18

money and credit cards were still there. That's why she called this

reporter. "I want people to know that _____ city that never sleeps
19

has _____ heart," Ms. Collins told us.
20

2. Nouns and Determiners

every + singular	*another* + singular	*this/that* + singular
each + singular	another person	this/that child
every father		
each father	*other* + plural	*these/those* + plural
	other people	these/those children
all + plural		
all fathers		

*Read this paragraph about people's attitudes towards crime. If the words in **bold** print are correct, put a check (✓) above them. If they are not correct, cross them out and write the correct words. There are five more errors. Compare your answers with a partner's.*

When people discuss their attitudes towards crime, you usually find

these

~~**this three kinds**~~ of people. There are some people who never question

police actions. They think we need more prisons and feel that **each laws**

should be stricter. Then there are **another people** who are the exact

opposite. They do not trust the police at all and sometimes prefer to

believe the criminals. Between **this two extreme positions** are those

people who try to understand the reasons for crime. **These reasons** can

be unemployment, drugs, poverty, neglect, or lack of education. When

every men and women believes it is important to give **all child** equal

opportunities, we can improve lives. Then we may have less crime.

E. Preparing the Final Draft

Reread your second draft and correct any errors you find. Put a check (✓) in each space as you edit for the points below. Then write your corrected final version.

CHECKLIST FOR EDITING THE SECOND DRAFT

_____ **articles**

_____ **nouns and determiners**

Additional Writing Opportunities

Choose one of the following topics:

1. Compare two friends or two members of your family. What are their similarities and differences? Write two paragraphs.

2. Read a newspaper in your native language and a newspaper in English. Compare and contrast the two newspapers. What are the similarities and differences? Write two paragraphs.

3. How do you find out about the news? Do you prefer newspapers, radio news, television news, or online news? Write a paragraph explaining your preference.

4. Listen to a radio or television news program in English. Take notes on the main stories. Write a summary of the news.

5. Write a paragraph about cheating. In your opinion, is cheating always wrong? Why or why not? Is copying homework cheating? What about cheating on a test in school? Why do some students do it? Is cheating ever justified? What is the punishment for cheating in your school?

9 FABLES FOR OUR TIME

WRITING A STORY

In this unit you will practice:
- writing a narrative of events
- working with theme, characters, and setting

Editing focus:
- simple past tense
- time clauses
- prepositions
- quotation marks

 I ## Fluency Practice: Freewriting

Many small children are afraid of the dark. Some are scared of monsters under the bed. Others are frightened of being alone. When you were a child, what were you afraid of? Did you ever have bad dreams? Did your parents or grandparents help you? Did they tell stories before you went to bed? What kinds of stories did you like?

Write for ten minutes about your childhood fears. Try to express yourself as well as you can. Don't worry about mistakes. Share your writing with a partner.

Here are some expressions you may want to use:

I was frightened of . . .	Monsters were frightening to me.
I was scared of . . .	Dark places were scary for me.
I was afraid of . . .	

II ▶ Reading for Writing

Storytelling is as old as human culture. In the past, most people did not know how to read. Storytellers would travel from village to village. Their stories were told for adults, but today we consider them children's stories. Here are two versions of a familiar folktale.[1] The first version was written down by the Grimm brothers in Germany in the 19th century, but the story itself is much older. The second is a modern version of the same story written by the American humorist James Thurber. Which one do you like better?

VERSION 1

LITTLE RED RIDING HOOD
Adapted from the Grimm Brothers' story

Once upon a time there was a sweet little girl who was loved by all who knew her. One day her mother told her to take some cakes and wine to her grandmother's house in the woods, but not to leave the path. That was too dangerous.

When Little Red Riding Hood reached the woods, she met a wolf who asked her where she was going. Little Red Riding Hood did not know what a wicked animal he was, so she was not afraid of him. She told the wolf all about her grandmother and where she lived. The wolf said, "Look at all the pretty flowers, Red Riding Hood. You don't even stop to hear the birds sing. You are as serious as if you were going to school." When Little Red Riding Hood saw the sunlight dancing through the trees and all the bright flowers, she thought, "I'm sure Grandmother would like some flowers." While Little Red Riding Hood was picking flowers, the wolf entered her grandmother's house and ate her up. He dressed in the grandmother's nightgown and nightcap and got into bed.

When Little Red Riding Hood got to her grandmother's house, she was surprised to see that the door was open. Everything seemed so strange. Even her grandmother looked very odd.[2]

"Oh, Grandmother," she said, "what big ears you have."

"The better to hear you with, my dear," said the wolf.

"Grandmother, what big eyes you have."

"The better to see you with."

"Grandmother, what big teeth you have."

"The better to eat you with!"

And the wolf sprang out[3] of bed and swallowed up Little Red Riding Hood. When the wolf satisfied himself, he fell asleep and snored[4] very loudly.

A huntsman went past the house, and hearing the loud snores, he decided to check on the old woman. When the hunter saw the wolf, he took his knife and cut open the wolf's stomach. Little Red Riding Hood and her grandmother jumped out. The wolf was dead and Little Red Riding Hood thought to herself, "My mother was right. I will never again go off the forest path when she tells me not to." And everyone lived happily ever after.

[1]A *folktale* is an old story, whose author is unknown, that is told from generation to generation. A *fairy tale* is a folktale with magical beings, such as fairies and witches. A *fable* is a story with animals who speak and act like humans. A fable has a clear moral or meaning written at the end. Some famous fables were written in ancient Greece by Aesop.
[2]*odd:* strange, weird
[3]*sprang out:* past tense of *spring out;* jumped out
[4]*snored:* breathed noisily through the nose and mouth while sleeping

VERSION 2

THE LITTLE GIRL AND THE WOLF
by James Thurber

One afternoon, a big wolf waited in the dark forest for a little girl to come along carrying a basket of food for her grandmother. Finally, a little girl did come along and she was carrying a basket of food. "Are you carrying a basket to your grandmother?" asked the wolf. The little girl said yes, she was. So the wolf asked her where her grandmother lived and the little girl told him and he disappeared into the woods.

When the little girl opened the door of her grandmother's house, she saw that there was somebody in bed with a nightcap and a nightgown on. She approached no nearer than 25 feet from the wolf, for even in a nightcap, a wolf doesn't look any more like your grandmother than the MGM lion[1] looks like Calvin Coolidge.[2] So the little girl took an automatic[3] out of her basket and shot the wolf dead.

Moral: It is not so easy to fool little girls nowadays as it used to be.

[1]*MGM:* the movie studio, Metro-Goldwyn-Mayer, has a lion as its symbol. The lion roars at the beginning of each film.
[2]*Calvin Coolidge:* a president of the United States in the 1920s
[3]*an automatic:* a machine gun that fires bullets automatically

A. General Understanding

1. The Traditional Story

What happened when? Use this list of events from Version 1 of the story to fill in the narrative chain of events.

- Red Riding Hood didn't recognize the wolf.

- Red Riding Hood picked flowers.

- The wolf tried to kill Little Red Riding Hood, but a hunter killed him.

- The wolf dressed up in the grandmother's clothes.

- The wolf killed the grandmother.

LITTLE RED RIDING HOOD

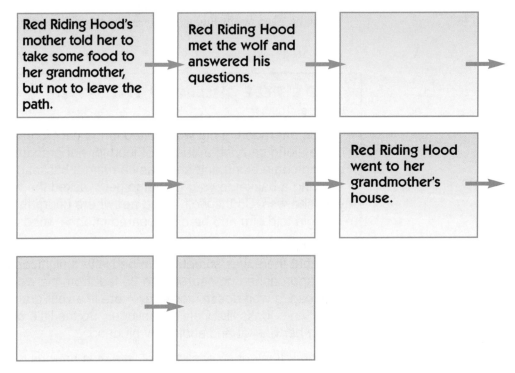

Fill in the blanks.

Setting: the woods
Time: the past

Characters: Little Red Riding Hood

her mother

_____

_____

2. The Modern Story

What happened when? Use this list of events from Version 2 of the story to fill in the narrative chain of events.

- A girl finally came along.
- The girl recognized the wolf in her grandmother's clothes.
- The girl killed the wolf.
- The wolf killed the grandmother.

THE LITTLE GIRL AND THE WOLF

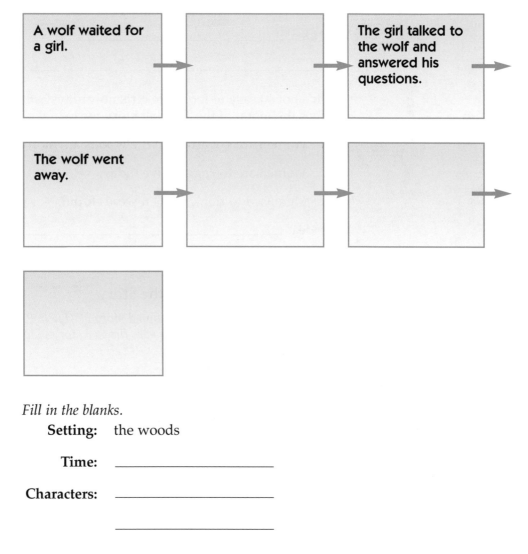

A wolf waited for a girl.		The girl talked to the wolf and answered his questions.

The wolf went away.		

Fill in the blanks.

Setting: the woods

Time: _____

Characters: _____

_____

B. Words and Ideas

1. The Moral of the Story

Read these questions and check (✓) the answers you agree with. Then write your own ideas. Discuss your answers with a partner.

1. What would be a good moral for the traditional story?

_____ A woman needs a man to save her.

_____ Little Red Riding Hood got what she deserved.

_____ Don't believe everything people tell you.

Your idea: _____

_____

2. "It's not so easy to fool little girls nowadays as it used to be." What does the moral of the Thurber story mean?

_____ Women are not afraid of the woods anymore.

_____ Women are too aggressive today.

_____ Men used to think women were stupid.

Your idea: _____

_____

2. Comparing Versions of the Story

With a partner, compare the traditional story of "Little Red Riding Hood" with the modern story by Thurber. How are the two stories similar? How are they different? Write your notes below.

Similarities	Differences

3. Which Story Do You Prefer?

Write a short paragraph explaining which story you prefer and why. Give at least three reasons. Use the notes you wrote in exercise 2. Read your paragraph to a partner.

I prefer the (traditional/modern) version of "Little Red Riding Hood"

because _____

_____

_____

_____

_____

_____

_____

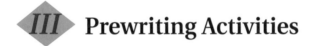

III ◆ Prewriting Activities

A. Children and Fairy Tales

Open for Discussion

Discuss these questions in a small group.

1. Some Americans do not like to read fairy tales to their children because they think the stories are cruel and frightening. What do you think?

2. Some people think that fairy tales are too old-fashioned and don't teach us about modern society. Do you agree or disagree?

3. Fairy tales try to teach important lessons. What are some of these lessons? Can you give examples from stories that you know?

4. Children can get hope for their future from the heroes of folktales. Do you agree or disagree? Give an example.

5. Do you or will you tell folktales and fairy tales to your children? If so, which ones?

B. Animals in Folktales

Dances with Wolves

Read these sentences. Write what you think each idiom means. Compare your answers with a partner's.

1. Business was terrible this month. Someone had to go to the board of directors and give them the bad news. We **threw** John **to the wolves** and made him go.

   We let him deliver the bad news by himself to save ourselves

   from an unpleasant meeting with the directors.

2. Slow down! Don't **wolf down** your food!

   _____

   _____

3. He's always chasing women and bothering them. He is **a wolf.**

   _____

   _____

4. Beware! He seems very gentle, but he's **a wolf in sheep's clothing.**

   _____

   _____

5. Don't call for help when you don't really need it because if you **cry wolf** too many times, people will never believe you again.

   _____

   _____

C. Optional Prewriting Task

Real wolves are not savage killers of men, but in western culture the wolf is a symbol of evil. What kinds of animals appear in the stories you know? Are they good or bad? Are they real animals or imaginary ones?

Write a short paragraph about the animals in the stories you know.

IV Structured Writing Focus

YOUR TASK

> Write your favorite folktale, fable, or fairy tale. It can be from your culture or from any other culture.
>
> ALTERNATIVE TASK: **Write a modern update of a folktale from your culture or any other culture.**

The Elements of a Story

All stories have some things in common.

Narrative

The narrative is the chain of events that tells the story. It is very important to tell the story in a logical way. Most stories are written in the **past tense** and the **third person.** ("She **told** the wolf all about **her** grandmother.")

Characters

The characters are clearly presented. **Descriptions** of the way they dress, the way they speak, or the way they look can give readers a better idea of the story.

Setting

The setting tells **when** and **where** the story is taking place, so that the readers can picture the time and place in their minds.

Theme and Moral

The theme is the **general topic** of the story. In "Little Red Riding Hood," one theme is how to keep safe in a dangerous world. The moral is the **lesson** of the story. The moral of the traditional story can be "Don't talk to strangers." The moral of the modern version can be "Don't try to fool girls any more."

WHAT IS AN UPDATE?

As people's ways of life and their values change, their stories change too. The basic elements stay the same, but some of the details change so that new generations can enjoy the stories.

Narrative

   a. Thurber kept the same general chain of events but left out parts not related to his moral.

   b. He kept the main characters of the story.

   c. He wrote in the past tense and the third-person singular.

Setting

    d. Thurber put in some aspects of modern life (the automatic).

Theme and Moral

    e. He changed the personality of Little Red Riding Hood so that she became more like a modern woman.

Match the traditional folktale on the left with its updated version on the right.

_____ 1. **The Frog Prince** (Europe)

Once upon a time, a princess was playing with her ball near a river. A frog caught the ball and said, "Kiss me. A witch's spell turned me into a frog, and only a woman's kiss can free me." The princess kissed him and the spell was broken. The princess and the prince lived happily ever after.

_____ 2. **The Idle Man and the Cow** (Korea)

Once upon a time, there was a farmer who was very lazy and hated his work. His wife yelled at him so much that he went to the market to escape. There he met an old man who sold him a cow mask. The old man said that this mask helped men who didn't want to work. When the farmer put the mask on his face he turned into a cow! The old man sold the cow. The cow had to work so hard and he was so lonely for his family that he wished he was dead. Suddenly, he changed back into a man. He rushed home and kissed his wife and children. From that day on, he was a good worker and he never saw the old man in the market again.

_____ 3. **The Odyssey** (Greece)

In ancient Greece, Homer wrote a long poem about this legend. Ulysses left his homeland to fight a ten-year war against the city of Troy. Then he spent ten more years trying to get back to his wife and son. Monsters attacked him, and the gods punished him. He got lost in storms and was kept a prisoner by beautiful goddesses. Finally, he was able to return to his family and his homeland.

a. Once there was a man who hated to work. All he wanted to do was drink with his friends. He was so lazy that his wife threw him out of the house. He thought his wife would forgive him as she always had. But this time, his wife took the children and went back to her mother. She finished college and got a good job and a nice house. The husband missed his family so much that he went to a clinic to stop drinking. He got a job and asked his wife if they could start a new life together. When she agreed, he became a good worker and was never lazy again.

b. Eusabio left his native country to come to America. He had to say good-bye to his wife and his parents. He came all alone and had a difficult journey. He couldn't find a place to live. He drove a taxi 14 hours a day, seven days a week. He had to learn English. It took a long time and a lot of work, but he finally got his green card. He sent money for his wife and parents to join him in America and live with him in a new house. He had found a new home.

c. Once upon a time, a very independent princess met a frog in a pond. The frog said, "One kiss from you and I will turn back into a prince. Then we can move into the castle with my mom where you can prepare my meals, clean my clothes, have my children, and forever feel lucky for doing so." That night the princess had frogs' legs for dinner.
Moral: You have to kiss a lot of frogs before you find a real prince.*

_____

*source: Recycled Paper Greetings, Inc.

A. Starting to Write

Brainstorming

Choose your story. Write the title below.

Title _____

IF YOU PLAN TO WRITE AN UPDATE

Make a list of the things you want to stay the same and the things you are going to change in your updated story.

What will stay the same?	What will change?

CHARACTERS

Write the names of the characters in your story. Make notes describing each character in an interesting way. (For example: wolf = ugly, smart, dangerous, charming?)

_____

_____

_____

CHAIN OF EVENTS

Write the chain of events for your story. You can use short notes. You don't have to write complete sentences or worry about grammar.

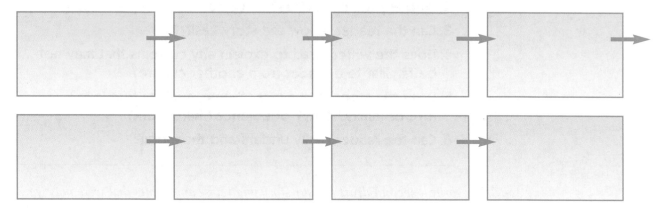

SETTING

Where: _____

When: _____

THEME AND MORAL

Theme: _____

Moral: _____

B. Preparing the First Draft

Using your notes, tell your story to a partner. Don't read it. You can also tape-record your voice. Then, discuss your story with a partner or listen to the tape you made. Consider these questions:

- Was the story clear?
- Was there any confusion in the chain of events?
- Was it easy to understand why the characters acted the way they did?
- Was the ending clear?

*After telling your story orally, write it as a **first draft.** Write complete sentences. Keep the story simple and put in only what is necessary. Try not to translate from your native language.*

C. Revising the First Draft

Read your story to a partner.

CHECKLIST FOR REVISING THE FIRST DRAFT

When you listen to your partner's story and discuss your own, keep these questions in mind:

1. What is the setting of the story? the time?

2. Who are the characters? Is it clear what they are doing?

3. Can the reader follow the story easily?

4. Does the writer need to explain any customs that may not be familiar to a reader from another culture?

5. Does the story have a clear theme, such as true love? love of family? duty? obedience? hard work?

6. Can the reader easily understand the moral?

---

*Now write a **second draft** of your story and revise any points that were not clear.*

D. Editing the Second Draft

After you have written your second draft, proofread your work to find any errors and correct them. These guidelines and exercises should help.

1. Practice with the Simple Past Tense

*Your stories should be written in the simple past tense. Read this story and look at the verbs in **bold** print. If the verb tense is correct, put a check (✓) above the verb. If it is not correct, cross out the verb and write the correct tense. There are ten more errors.*

Beauty and the Beast

Once upon a time, a merchant **lose** [*lost*] his way in a storm. He found an

empty castle in the woods and **spends** the night there. In the morning, he

taked a rose from the garden for his youngest daughter. All of a sudden, a

terrible Beast appeared. The merchant would have to stay in the Beast's

castle forever. The merchant **begs** for time to go home to say good-bye

to his family. When he got home and **told** his story, his daughter Beauty

decided to take his place and live with the Beast.

When Beauty **had arrived** at the Beast's castle, she was shocked by the

ugliness of the Beast. Every night the Beast **eats** dinner with Beauty and asked

her to marry him. She always refused. But Beauty soon learned to appreciate

the Beast's gentle ways. When Beauty **hears** that her father was ill, she asked

for permission to visit him. She promised to return to the Beast after a week.

When she **go** home, she took care of her father and **meets** many young men.

She realized that she really loved the Beast.

While Beauty was away, the Beast **began** to die. As soon as Beauty knew the Beast was dying, she **hurried** back to him and **say**, "Dearest Beast, you must be strong and live so that we may become man and wife, because I love you with all my heart." Love broke the spell and the Beast **turns** into a handsome Prince.

2. Time Clauses

Study these sentences:

1. **Before** he left, the merchant asked his daughters what they wanted.
2. **After** she heard her father's story, Beauty decided to take his place.
3. **While** Beauty was away, her father became ill.
4. **When** Beauty heard that her father was ill, she begged the Beast for permission to visit him.

Answer these questions about the sentences above.

1. In the first sentence, what happened first?

    a. The merchant asked his daughters a question.

    b. The merchant started his trip.

2. In the second sentence, what happened first?

    a. Beauty made a decision.

    b. The merchant talked to his daughter.

3. In the third sentence, what is the correct order of events?

    a. Beauty's father was ill before she went to the Beast's castle.

    b. Both events took place at the same time.

4. In the fourth sentence, what is the correct order of events?

    a. Both events happened at the same time.

    b. Her father became ill, and then Beauty asked to go home.

You can connect two events or actions in one sentence by using an adverb of time, such as these:

before   **when**
after   **while**

The two parts of the sentence below are in the simple past tense. When the adverb comes first, there is a comma between the two parts of the sentence.

Before he left, the merchant said good-bye to his daughters.

When the adverb is in the second part of the sentence, there is no comma. The meaning of the sentence is exactly the same.

The merchant said good-bye to his daughters **before** he left.

With a partner, combine the two sentences into one by using a time clause. Remember to use the simple past tense.

1. **when**

    The merchant comes home.

    He tells his daughters about his promise to the Beast.

When the merchant came home, he told his daughters about his promise to the Beast.

         or

The merchant told his daughters about his promise to the Beast when he came home.

2. **after**

    Beauty falls in love with the Beast.

    She takes the time to understand him.

    _____

3. **while**

    Beauty is away from the Beast.

    She realizes her true feelings.

    _____

4. **after**

    The Beast learns to be gentle and patient.

    He is ready to get married.

    _____

5. **when**

   Beauty learns to judge the goodness inside the Beast.
   She is ready for marriage.

   _____

6. **after**

   They live happily ever after.
   Beauty marries her prince.

   _____

3. Prepositions of Place

Prepositions of place show the location of people and objects.

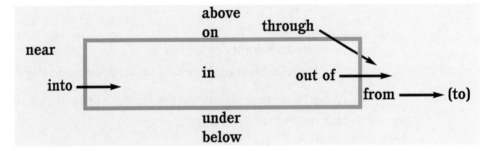

*In this paragraph from a student's version of "Moon Princess," the prepositions are in **bold** print. Put a check (✓) above the correct prepositions. If they are not correct, cross them out and write the correct ones. There are three more errors.*

This is a very famous Japanese story. When we were children, our

parents read us this story when we were (1) **in** bed. (2) ~~On~~ In an ancient

bamboo forest, on a mountain (3) **on** Japan, there lived an old bamboo

tree cutter and his wife. One day, when he cut down a bamboo tree, there

was a baby (4) **through** it. A golden light was shining (5) **on** her face and

they called her Moon Princess. After that, all the bamboo trees the cutter

found (6) **on** the forest were full of gold. The daughter grew up to be

beautiful and noble minded.

"Moon Princess" continues below. Fill in the blanks with the correct prepositions.

Hearing of her dazzling beauty, people came (7) _____ all parts of the country to see her, but she never married. One night, crying, the princess said, "Too soon! The moon people will come here on the fifteenth night of August to take me back to the moon. I must leave you on that night." The kind parents said, "We will hire a thousand samurai to protect you."

On the night of the full moon, when the sky was extremely clear and the moon shone like a polished mirror, the samurai stood (8) _____ the roof and (9) _____ the garden. As the full moon rose, the moon people came down (10) _____ earth. The samurai were suddenly paralyzed. They couldn't move or speak. The princess walked (11) _____ of the house and said, "Dear Old Parents, we may never meet again." Then Moon Princess rose up (12) _____ the sky and disappeared in the night.

4. Quotations

When you want your story to include a conversation, you need to use quotation marks.

The princess said, "Dear Old Parents, we may never meet again."
The princess said: "Dear Old Parents, we may never meet again."*

Use either a comma or a colon after "said." The first word of any quotation begins with a capital letter.

"Dear Old Parents, we may never meet again," said the princess.

When the quotation comes at the beginning of the sentence, use only a comma. Put it before the end of the quotation.

---

*You do not have to use the past tense inside the quotes.

Rewrite these sentences using correct punctuation.

1. you will pay for stealing the rose said the Beast

   <u>"You will pay for stealing the rose," said the Beast.</u>

2. dearest Beast you must be strong and live so that we can be husband and wife said Beauty

   _____

3. moon princess said I must leave you on that night

   _____

4. too soon she said

   _____

5. the kind parents said we will hire a thousand samurai to protect you

   _____

E. Preparing the Final Draft

Reread your second draft and correct any errors you find. Put a check (✓) in each space as you edit for the points below.

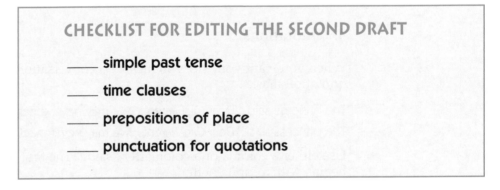

CHECKLIST FOR EDITING THE SECOND DRAFT

_____ simple past tense

_____ time clauses

_____ prepositions of place

_____ punctuation for quotations

Exchange papers with a partner and make sure that all the points were checked. Then write your corrected final version.

V Additional Writing Opportunities

Choose one of the following topics and write one or two paragraphs.

1. Compare these two versions of the same story. Discuss their similarities and differences. What lessons do these stories teach? Which story do you prefer and why?

The Princess and the Pea

Once upon a time, there was a prince who wanted to marry. His mother and father wanted him to marry a true princess. Every time the prince invited a girl to meet his family, they invited her to stay the night. The Prince's mother would put a hundred mattresses on the girl's bed and hide one little pea under everything. "If she is a true princess, the pea will hurt her soft skin and she will not be able to sleep," said the Queen. Many girls tried to marry the prince, but no one could pass the test.

Finally, the Prince brought home a girl who looked very poor. Her clothes were all torn. "She will never do," said the Prince's parents. But after one night in the bed with the hundred mattresses and the pea, the girl came to breakfast and said, "I couldn't sleep at all. Something must have been in my bed." She was the true princess! She married her prince and they lived happily ever after.

The Princess and the Bowling Ball

Once upon a time, there was a Prince. This Prince's Dad and Mom (the King and Queen) somehow got it into their royal heads that no Princess would be good enough for their boy unless she could feel a pea through a hundred mattresses. So it should come as no surprise that the Prince had a very hard time finding a Princess. Every time he met a nice girl, his Mom and Dad would pile one hundred mattresses on top of a pea and then invite her to sleep over.

When the Princess came down for breakfast, the Queen would say, "How did you sleep, dear?" The Princess would politely say, "Fine, thanks." And the King would show her the door.

Now this went on for three years, and, of course, no one ever felt a pea under a hundred mattresses. Then one day the Prince met the girl of his dreams. He decided he had better do something about it. That night, before the Princess went to bed, he slipped a bowling ball under the hundred mattresses.

When the Princess came to breakfast the next morning, the Queen asked, "How did you sleep, dear?" "This might sound odd," said the Princess, "but I think you need another mattress. I felt like I was sleeping on a lump as big as a bowling ball."

The King and Queen were satisfied. The Prince and the Princess were married. And everyone lived happily, although maybe not completely honestly, ever after.

From *The Stinky Cheese Man* by Jon Scieszka and Lane Smith.

2. Do you think that children should read or listen to fairy tales and traditional stories? Are the stories cruel and too scary? Will you tell these stories to your children? If not, what other kinds of stories will you tell them?

3. The study of fairy tales can be extended to TV shows, movie videos, and plays. Here are some examples:

- *Ever After*: a retelling of the Cinderella story where Cinderella has the personality of a modern girl
- *Wolf:* a modern retelling of the werewolf myth
- *Mulan:* the Disney version of an old Chinese story
- *Ladyhawke:* a new story situated in the Middle Ages in the style of a fairy tale
- *Beauty and the Beast:* the U.S. television version available on video where Beauty is a lawyer and the Beast lives in the tunnels under New York City
- *Beauty and the Beast*: the Disney version of this story
- *Once upon a Mattress*: a musical play based on the story of "The Princess and the Pea"

Watch a video or film retelling of a fairy tale. How was it similar to the traditional story? How was it different? Did you like it? Why or why not?

10 WHAT I HAVE LIVED FOR

Bertrand Russell

In this unit you will practice:
- organizing an essay
- writing a thesis statement

Editing focus:
- present perfect tense
- future time clauses
- adjective and adverb word forms
- noun and verb word forms

I Fluency Practice: Freewriting

The Roman emperor Marcus Aurelius wrote:

"Remember this, that very little is needed to have a happy life."

Do you think this statement is true? In your opinion, what does a person need in order to have a happy life? Can a poor person have as happy a life as a rich person?

Write for ten minutes to explain your opinion. Try to express yourself as well as you can. Don't worry about mistakes. Share your writing with a partner.

II Reading for Writing

This essay was written by Bertrand Russell, one of the great mathematicians, philosophers, and writers of the 20th century. He was born in 1872 into a rich and noble British family. He wrote *Principia Mathematica, A History of Western Philosophy*, and many other works. Russell won the Nobel Prize in literature in 1950. In 1958 Lord Russell began the first of his many campaigns for nuclear disarmament of both the United States and the former Soviet Union. He died at the age of 98.

WHAT I HAVE LIVED FOR

Three passions, simple but overwhelmingly strong,[1] have governed my life: the longing for love, the search for knowledge, and unbearable[2] pity for the suffering of mankind.

I have sought[3] love, first, because it brings ecstasy—ecstasy so great that I would often have sacrificed all the rest of life for a few hours of this joy. I have sought it, next, because it relieves loneliness. I have sought it, finally, because in the union of love, I have seen the vision of the heaven that saints and poets have imagined. That is what I have sought, and though it may seem too good for human life, this is what—at last—I have found.

With equal passion, I have sought knowledge. I have wished to understand the hearts of men. I have wished to know why the stars shine. And I have tried to understand the Pythagorean power[4] by which numbers hold sway above the flux.[5] A little of this, but not much, I have achieved.

Love and knowledge, so far as they were possible, led upward toward the heavens. But always pity brought me back to earth. Echoes of cries of pain reverberate[6] in my heart. Children in famine,[7] victims tortured by oppressors, helpless old people a hated burden to their sons, and the whole world of loneliness, poverty, and pain make a mockery of what human life should be. I long to alleviate[8] the evil, but I cannot, and I too suffer.

This has been my life. I have found it worth living, and would gladly live it again if the chance were offered me.

---

[1]*overwhelmingly strong:* very strong, almost out of control
[2]*unbearable:* so painful or unpleasant that a person can't stand it
[3]*sought:* past tense of *seek;* looked for
[4]*Pythagorean power:* the power of numbers. Pythagoras, an ancient Greek, developed geometry, one of the first serious studies of mathematics
[5]*". . . understand the Pythagorean power by which numbers hold sway over the flux.":* to understand how mathematics can provide the key to nature's laws
[6]*reverberate:* echo
[7]*famine:* extreme hunger, starvation
[8]*alleviate:* relieve (suffering), cure

A. General Understanding

Mark these statements true (T) or false (F).

_____ 1. Bertrand Russell felt that romantic love could give him an idea of heaven.

_____ 2. Russell said that his search for love was successful.

_____ 3. Russell found all the knowledge he was looking for.

_____ 4. Bertrand Russell felt sympathy for people who suffered.

_____ 5. Russell was pleased with his life.

B. Words and Ideas

1. Explaining the Meaning

Write your answers to these questions. Share your answers with a partner. Different explanations are possible.

1. Bertrand Russell says that "love and knowledge . . . led upward toward the heavens." What does he mean?

   _____

   _____

2. What does Russell mean when he says, "always pity brought me back to earth"?

   _____

   _____

3. Why do you think Bertrand Russell wanted "to understand the hearts of men"?

   _____

   _____

4. Why can't Russell cure all the evils he sees in society?

   _____

   _____

5. What aspects of life does Russell not talk about? What kinds of things are not part of his three passions?

_____

_____

_____

_____

2. Summarizing

For each paragraph (¶) of Russell's essay, write a one-sentence summary in your own words. Share your summaries with the class.

¶1 The three most important things in Bertrand Russell's life were love, knowledge, and pity.

_____

¶2 Love gave him joy and protection against loneliness, and it helped him understand heaven.

_____

¶3

_____

¶4

_____

¶5

_____

III ◆ Prewriting Activities

A. Time Lines

1. Bertrand Russell's Life

This is a time line of some of the most important events in Bertrand Russell's life.

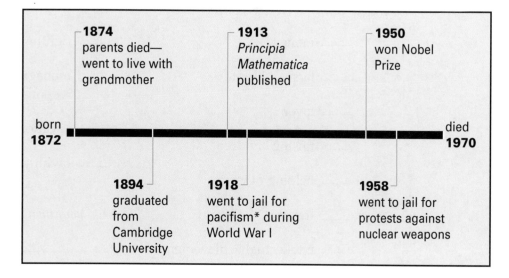

2. Your Life

On this time line, write the most important or the most interesting events in your life so far. Share them with a partner.

---

*pacifism: Russell did not agree with either side in World War I, and he was put in jail for refusing to fight. He did participate in World War II to defeat Nazism.

B. What's Most Important?

Circle the five things that are most important to you in your life. Then number them from 1 to 5, with "1" being the most important. Compare your answers with a partner's. Do you think your choices will change as you grow older? How?

———— happiness

———— money

———— husband/wife

———— lover

———— raising children

———— helping others

———— travel

———— intellectual achievement

———— good job

———— peace of mind

———— moral behavior

———— helping the poor

———— fighting injustice

———— managing your responsibilities

———— vacations

———— owning your own house

Add your own choices.

———— ————————————————

———— ————————————————

———— ————————————————

———— ————————————————

IV Structured Writing Focus

YOUR TASK

Write an essay of at least three paragraphs about what you live for. What is important to you? What are your hopes for the future? What have you accomplished in your life?

ALTERNATIVE TASK: **Write about someone that you know well. What does that person live for? What are his or her hopes and dreams? What has that person accomplished?**

A. Starting to Write

Brainstorming

Use the work you have done on pages 145, 149, and 150 to start thinking about your essay. Write your notes here. You do not have to write complete sentences or worry about grammar.

_____

_____

_____

_____

_____

_____

_____

_____

_____

_____

_____

B. Preparing the First Draft

1. Essay Structure

Reread Bertrand Russell's essay. Study the essay structure, using the information in the margins as a guide. Then with a partner, answer the questions that follow.

What I Have Lived For

¶1
Introduction

Three passions, simple but overwhelmingly strong, have governed my life: the longing for love, the search for knowledge, and unbearable pity for the suffering of mankind. ← **Thesis Statement**

¶2
Body
(Love)

I have sought love, first, because it brings ecstasy—ecstasy so great that I would often have sacrificed all the rest of life for a few hours of this joy. I have sought it, next, because it relieves loneliness. I have sought it, finally, because in the union of love, I have seen the vision of the heaven that saints and poets have imagined. That is what I have sought, and though it may seem too good for human life, this is what—at last—I have found. ← **Topic Sentence**

Support

← **Concluding Sentence**

¶3
Body
(Knowledge)

With equal passion, I have sought knowledge. I have wished to understand the hearts of men. I have wished to know why the stars shine. And I have tried to understand the Pythagorean power by which numbers hold sway above the flux. A little of this, but not much, I have achieved.

¶4
Body
(Pity)

Love and knowledge, so far as they were possible, led upward toward the heavens. But always pity brought me back to earth. Echoes of cries of pain reverberate in my heart. Children in famine, victims tortured by oppressors, helpless old people a hated burden to their sons, and the whole world of loneliness, poverty, and pain make a mockery of what human life should be. I long to alleviate the evil, but I cannot, and I too suffer. ← **Topic Sentence***

¶5
Conclusion

This has been my life. I have found it worth living, and would gladly live it again if the chance were offered me.

---

*The first sentence in paragraph 4 is *not* the topic sentence. It is a transitional sentence summarizing the main ideas of paragraphs 2 and 3. The topic sentence of paragraph 4 is the second sentence.

1. How does the first paragraph show that the three topics of the body of this essay will be love, knowledge, and pity?

2. Why does this essay have five paragraphs?

3. Underline the topic sentence in paragraph 3.

4. Compare the tone of the first two sentences in paragraph 4. (*Tone* means how the sentences make you feel when you read them.)

5. Write the words *support* and *concluding sentence* where they belong for paragraphs 3 and 4.

2. Thesis Statement

WHY IS THE THESIS STATEMENT IMPORTANT?

- The thesis statement communicates the **main idea** of an essay and tells the reader what the author is going to show or prove.

- The thesis statement tells the **topic of each paragraph** in the body of the essay.

"Three passions, simple but overwhelmingly strong, have governed my life: the longing for **love,** the search for **knowledge,** and unbearable **pity** for the suffering of mankind."

| paragraph 2 Love | paragraph 3 Knowledge | paragraph 4 Pity |

With a partner, read the following thesis statements. What should the topics of the body paragraphs be? How many paragraphs should each essay have?

1. Without a doubt, his key to a happy life was having a challenging job and good friends to enjoy his leisure time with.

   Number of paragraphs in the essay:

   <u>4 (introduction, 2 body paragraphs, conclusion)</u>

   Topic(s) of the body paragraph(s):

   <u>job, friends</u>

2. His father's philosophy focused on the joys of family life, the importance of being self-confident, and the benefits of a good education.

   Number of paragraphs in the essay: _____

   Topic(s) of the body paragraph(s): _____

3. My goal in life is to become the best possible parent to my children by giving them unconditional love.

   Number of paragraphs in the essay: _____

   Topic(s) of the body paragraph(s): _____

WRITING YOUR OWN THESIS STATEMENT AND ORGANIZING YOUR IDEAS

Review the notes that you wrote in the Brainstorming section on page 151. Then organize your notes here.

Title _____

Introduction

Thesis Statement _____

Body

How many paragraphs will you need to explain this thesis? _____
Divide your notes into the number of paragraphs you need.

Conclusion

---

*Write a **first draft** of your essay. Write complete sentences. Try to use some of the vocabulary and structures you have seen in this unit. Make sure your thesis statement is as clear as possible.*

C. Revising the First Draft

Read your essay to a partner.

CHECKLIST FOR REVISING THE FIRST DRAFT

When you read a partner's essay and discuss your own, keep these points in mind:

1. Does the essay give an interesting picture of the writer's life, hopes, dreams, and achievements?

2. Is the thesis statement clear?

3. Does each body paragraph develop a part of the thesis?

4. Does each body paragraph have good examples and support?

5. Is there a concluding paragraph for the essay?

After you have discussed your essay with a partner, you may want to improve your thesis statement or add more ideas to the body paragraphs. Some reorganization may be necessary. Reread your essay aloud to yourself.

*Now write a **second draft** that includes all the additions and changes.*

D. Editing the Second Draft

After you have written a second draft, proofread your work to find any errors and correct them. These guidelines and exercises should help.

1. The Present Perfect Tense

With a partner, study these sentences and answer the questions that follow.

> I **sought** knowledge.
> I **seek** knowledge.
> I **have sought** knowledge.

1. Which sentence tells us about an action that is taking place now?
2. Which sentence tells us about an action that took place in the past?
3. Which sentence tells us about an action that started in the past and is still taking place in the present?

The **present tense** refers to an action that is taking place now.

I **seek** knowledge.

The **simple past tense** refers to an action that took place in the past.

I **sought** knowledge.

The **present perfect tense** refers to an action that started in the past and continues in the present.

I **have sought** knowledge.

This sentence means:
1. I began to seek knowledge some time in the past.
2. I still seek knowledge today.

Words and expressions like *all my life, since I was a child, since January, for ten years,* and *recently* are used with the present perfect tense.

To form the present perfect tense, follow this pattern:
auxiliary *have* + the past participle of the verb

have	**sought**
HAVE	PAST PARTICIPLE

I **have**	always	**sought** knowledge.
HAVE	ADVERB	PAST PARTICIPLE

Fill in the blanks in these sentences with the correct forms of the present perfect tense. Compare your answers with a partner's.

1. I _____ (understand) the nature of loneliness since the

   death of my father on April 18, 1999.

2. Since he died, expressions of sympathy from my family and friends

   _____ (help) to alleviate the pain.

3. My mother herself _____ (suffer) a great deal during

   this period of mourning.

4. Both she and I _____ (find) some relief in our grief.

5. In the past year, we _____ (become) closer to each other.

With a partner, complete the paragraph with the correct forms of the present tense, the simple past tense, or the present perfect tense of the verb.

I ___became___ (become) a teacher in September 1988. At the very

beginning, I _____ (learn) that teaching is not a simple job.

But I also _____ (know), even then, that doing something

worthwhile is never easy. Through the years, my students

_____ (teach) me that my efforts _____ (guide)

many of them on the road to success. In fact, when I meet some of my

former students today, I _____ (see) my own success as a

teacher in their successful careers. I am glad that, over the years, I

_____ (always try) to do my best.

2. Future Time Clauses

With a partner, read these sentences and answer the questions that follow.

Before I retire, I **will study** the needs of my community.
When I retire, I **will do** volunteer work in my community.
I **will work** with the elderly in my community **after** I retire.*

1. When will the writer study the needs of the community?
2. What will he do after he retires?

Future Time Clauses

The sentences above look from the past to the future. They all tell what
<u>will happen</u> (future tense) when, after, or before something else <u>happens</u>
(present tense).

when			
after	+	present tense	future tense
before			

*Fill in the correct tenses of the verbs in these sentences. Compare your answers
with a partner's.*

1. I hope I ____will meet____ *(meet)* my true love before I get

   too unhappy.

2. After I _____ *(find)* love, I _____ *(be)*

   ecstatic.

3. When this _____ *(happen)*, all my feelings of loneliness

   _____ *(disappear)*.

4. In addition, I _____ *(feel)* happier when I

   _____ *(be)* brave enough to declare my love for

   another person.

---

*When the clauses are in reverse order, there is no comma separating the
two parts of the sentence.

Complete each of these sentences with at least four different endings. Share what you write with a partner.

I will be happy after I hand in my paper.

_____

_____

_____

_____

The world will be a better place when _____

_____

_____

_____

_____

3. Word Forms

Adjectives and Adverbs

Adverbs describe or modify verbs. They show how an action is done.

The man **answered** the question **joyfully.**

adjective	+	-ly	=	adverb
joyful	+	-ly	=	joyfully
horrible	+	-ly	=	horribly

Write the correct form of the adverb next to each of the following adjectives.

Adjectives	Adverbs
glad	_____
helpless	_____
overwhelming	_____
terrible	_____
unbearable	_____

Verbs and Nouns

verb	+	*-ing*	=	noun
suffer	+	*-ing*	=	suffering
understand	+	*-ing*	=	understanding
verb	+	*-ment*	=	noun
govern	+	*-ment*	=	government

Take away verb ending		Add noun ending	=	noun
relie~~ve~~	+	*-f*	=	relief
allevi~~ate~~	+	*-ation*	=	alleviation

noun	+	*-ize*	=	verb
victim	+	*-ize*	=	victimize

Study these verbs and nouns:

Verbs	**Nouns**
understand	understanding
alleviate	alleviation
relieve	relief
victimize	victim
govern	government
suffer	suffering

Use the correct forms of the nouns, verbs, adjectives, and adverbs listed on pages 159–160 to fill in the blanks in these paragraphs.

In history, people who have criticized their **g**<u>overnment</u> have often **s**_____ a great deal. Bertrand Russell experienced a little of this **t**_____ fate when he criticized both Britain and Britain's enemies' participation in World War I (1914–1918). He became a **v**_____ of the laws against pacifists: He was forced to pay a fine, he went to jail, and he lost his job at Cambridge University. However, despite the often **un**_____ conditions in prison, Russell did

a lot of work. He wrote a book in jail called *Introduction to Mathematical*

Philosophy, which received an **o**_____ positive response at

the university.

    After Russell left prison, he traveled around the world. He continued

to seek **r**_____ for all people who were **v**_____

by injustice. He tried to **a**_____ the pain of human

s_____ through his books and his actions. The fact that he

gl_____ sacrificed his comforts in order to do the right thing

was obvious even when he was a very old man. At 89 he went to jail again

for participating in an antinuclear demonstration with people young

enough to be his great-grandchildren.

E. Preparing the Final Draft

Reread your second draft and correct any errors you find. Put a check (✓) in each
space as you edit for the points below. Then write your corrected final version.

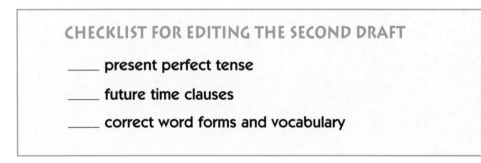

CHECKLIST FOR EDITING THE SECOND DRAFT

_____ **present perfect tense**

_____ **future time clauses**

_____ **correct word forms and vocabulary**

Additional Writing Opportunities

Choose one of the following topics and write an essay.

1. Bertrand Russell believed that pacifism was the best way to resolve most international conflicts. Do you think pacifism is a good way to resolve the problems of this world, or do you think that violence is sometimes necessary?

2. "It is the possibility of having a dream come true that makes life interesting."—Paul Coelho

   What does this quote mean? Do you have a dream? Is your life more interesting because you are trying to make your dream come true?

3. Have you ever had an opinion that was different from everybody else's opinion? Did this occur in school or in your family or among friends? What happened? Did you defend your ideas well, or were you overwhelmed by other people? What do you think about this experience now?

4. "What do we live for, if it is not to make the world less difficult for each other?"—George Eliot

   What does this quote mean? Why is the world so difficult? Should we try to make life easier for people we love? for people we work with? for strangers? Do you agree or disagree with this quote?

SUPPLEMENTARY ACTIVITIES

These suggestions come from our own classes and the classes of our colleagues.

UNIT 1
GETTING ACQUAINTED

Photo collage

1. Have students ask for a photo of the partner they have interviewed, or take pictures of students in class. Students can also ask their partners to bring pictures or small items that reflect their personalities and interests. Display the photos with the students' paragraphs in the classroom to create a more personal atmosphere and to reinforce the notion of the writing class as a "community."

Oral report

2. Have students research one of the famous people whose picture is found in this unit, or a celebrity of their choice. Each student can give a brief oral report to the class or to a small group. Encourage students to ask at least one question per report.

Debate

3. To improve listening and speaking skills and/or to prepare for another writing activity, hold a class debate for and against horror movies. Maintain time limits. Have one student keep track of time, and give each team a time limit to present its arguments for the debate. After each team has presented its arguments, give the other team a time limit within which to respond.

   For additional writing practice, teams can list their ideas for arguments. They can also take notes while the other team presents its arguments.

Writing about films

4. Provide a short list of horror movies and have students write a review of one of them, making sure that at least two students write about the same film. Then have the students exchange and compare their reviews. They can respond in writing to each other's review.

5. Have students write a short comparison of two horror movies: one from the past and one from the present. Suggestions for comparisons include *Nosferatu* (1922) and *Dracula* (1992), and *The Wolf Man* (1941) and *Wolf* (1994).

UNIT 2
WHO IS A HERO?

Listening

1. Use the short paragraphs about Martin Luther King, Jr., as dictation or for listening comprehension practice.

2. Have students read passages from Martin Luther King's speech "I Have a Dream." Then play King's speech on audiocassette several times. (The audio recording is commonly available in libraries.) Have students take notes the second and third time and then compare their notes. Open a discussion with questions such as "Why is King a hero in contemporary America?"

Film discussion

3. Show a film about a person with a disability who has overcome many obstacles. You can select some scenes or show the entire film in segments. Suggested films are *The Miracle Worker* (1962) and *Rain Man* (1988).

   The Miracle Worker tells the real-life story of Hellen Keller and Anne Sullivan. Have students read about Keller and Sullivan before watching the film. After the film, discuss the characters and their actions. Ask students, "Which one of these characters is a hero, or are both? What criteria define a hero?"

   Rain Man explores the relationship between two brothers, one of whom is autistic. Have students compare the brothers and decide if either is a hero. Ask students, "What are heroic acts?"

   Other possible films for discussion are *Born on the Fourth of July* (1989) and *The Other Side of the Mountain* (1975).

UNIT 3
WEATHERING THE STORM

Oral report

1. Have students give two-minute reports on natural disasters that they have researched or experienced, such as hurricanes, earthquakes, and volcanic eruptions. They can also report on catastrophes such as the sinking of the *Titanic*. Reports can be given in small groups. Encourage students to ask at least one question per presentation.

Film discussion

2. Show excerpts from natural-disaster films. Have the students take notes describing the unleashing of the elements. Suggested films include *Twister* (1996), *The Perfect Storm* (2000), and *Earthquake* (1974).

Impromptu speeches

3. Have students draw topics from a hat and give an impromptu one-minute speech on their topic. (You may want to model a speech for them first.) You could also have students write the topics themselves. Possible topics include how to ride a bike, how to dance, and how to carve a turkey.

UNIT 4
THE BABY JESSICA CASE

Internet research

1. Have students research the Baby Jessica case on the Internet. They can work in pairs to find out if updated information on the DeBoers and the Schmidts is available. Students can summarize their findings in a paragraph or in a discussion.

Writing about films

2. Show a small part of the film *Losing Isaiah* (1995), which examines an interracial adoption case in which the birth mother wants her child back. The film ends with a compromise between the two mothers. Have students write a personal response to the film and/or to the issues involved. Before showing the end of the film, have students write about what they think should happen to Isaiah. After viewing the end of the film, they can think about whether the solution in this film could have worked in the Baby Jessica case.

UNIT 5
THE GREATEST INVENTION OF THE 20TH CENTURY

Listening

1. Record the paragraph on Alexander Fleming to use as a dictation or listening comprehension exercise. The interview with Marconi can be recorded with two voices. This exercise makes an excellent cloze in which students fill in the correct verb forms as they hear them.

2. Show a few scenes from the film *Pirates of Silicon Valley* (1999), which dramatizes the lives of Steve Jobs (inventor of Apple/Macintosh) and Bill Gates (of Microsoft). The film can be used as a listening comprehension exercise. Students can write about the qualities these men possess. Alternatively, have students research other leading inventors or entrepreneurs for a future class discussion or report.

UNIT 6
HOME SWEET HOME

Matching descriptions

1. Have students bring photographs or illustrations of the rooms they have described in this unit. Photocopy the pictures and the written descriptions for students to match. This activity can be done as a whole class or in groups.

Listening

2. Use the passage about Frank Lloyd Wright as a listening comprehension or dictation exercise.

Field trip

3. Take your class on a trip to a museum or design center where they can describe rooms, furniture, jewelry, clothes, or other objects by using prepositions to indicate spatial positions. To make the best use of museum time, prior to the trip, have students choose which room or which objects they will describe. (Show them a map or index first.) You can also have students take notes at the museum and write their paragraphs later. If no museum is available, students can describe particular areas of their university, college, or high school campus.

Describing and responding to art

4. Have students choose from several reproductions of paintings by various artists (e.g., Georgia O'Keeffe, Andrew Pollack, Magritte, and Picasso) and write a personal response in their journals or in class. You can also have students write descriptions of the art. Students can then read each other's writing. This activity works particularly well when students have written on some of the same works of art.

Walking tour

5. Have students organize an architectural walking tour of the school's neighborhood or campus. To practice with prepositions of place, have students write a walking tour guide for their campus.

UNIT 7
A MOUSE GOES TO PARIS

Restaurant survey

1. Have students publish their own restaurant guide based on a survey they conduct. Ask the class to write a list of restaurants in the area and specific topics for the survey, such as food, cost, and atmosphere. Then have students visit selected restaurants in groups or pairs and write their evaluations of each restaurant. Collect and photocopy the reports, and assemble them as a booklet titled "Student Restaurant Guide." Publishing student writing gives it added value and greater meaning for the group.

UNIT 8
THE CRIME THAT DIDN'T HAPPEN

Matching headlines

1. Create exercises in which students must match current headlines with newspaper stories.

Comparing crime stories

2. Have students read two versions of a crime story covered in different newspapers. Then have them discuss the differences between the versions or write a comparison.

3. Show scenes from two crime films, one from the past and one from the present. Have students write comparisons of the characters, settings, plots, or the use of violence.

Comic strip stories

4. Photocopy newspaper comics with the words in the speech bubbles removed. Have students supply their own words in the speech bubbles, based on their interpretations of the comic strip's plot. They can compare their work with a partner's and then share their stories with the class.

UNIT 9
FABLES FOR OUR TIME

Writing and discussing fairy tales

1. Have students write fairy tales or legends from their cultures; then collect and photocopy the final drafts and assemble them as a small booklet titled "Stories from All over the World."

2. Have students select and read other fables by James Thurber from his collection, *Fables for Our Time*. Students may also be interested in Thurber's short stories "The Unicorn in the Garden" and "The Secret Life of Walter Mitty."

3. Have students read the didactic *Fables and Fairy Tales* by Leo Tolstoy (translated into English) or the humorous collection *Politically Correct Bedtime Stories* by James Finn Garner. Read these as a class or prepare them on audiocassette as a listening comprehension exercise.

UNIT 10
WHAT I HAVE LIVED FOR

Time lines

1. Have one or two students research Bertrand Russell and report to the class on his achievements and his life. They can draw a more detailed time line of his life on the board. (This activity will help students distinguish the simple past and past perfect tenses.) Students can also research other historical figures and then summarize their biographies in time lines or in written paragraphs.

Family history research

2. Have students research their own family history, summarize it in paragraphs, and draw a time line of events or a genealogical tree. (You may want to provide a model first.)

Historical research

3. Have students investigate the history of pacifism in the United States or in other countries and consider questions such as *What are the religious roots of pacifism? Is pacifism a valid reason for being excused from military service? Does the United States government excuse pacifists from military service?*

ENDNOTES
FAMOUS PEOPLE (PAGE 4)

The famous people are:

a. **Chief Sitting Bull** (1831–1890): leader of the Lakota Sioux; defeated General Custer at the Battle of the Little Bighorn (1876).

b. **Mary Wollstonecraft Shelley** (1797–1851): English author of *Frankenstein*; wife of the romantic poet Percy Shelley.

c. **Charles Darwin** (1809–1882): English naturalist; developed the theory of evolution in *Origin of the Species*.

d. **Abraham Lincoln** (1809–1865): 16th president of the United States; freed the slaves during the American Civil War (1861–1865).

e. **Albert Einstein** (1879–1955): German-born American physicist; developed the theory of relativity. Einstein won the Nobel Prize in physics in 1921.

f. **Virginia Woolf** (1882–1941): English author and feminist; wrote the famous essay *A Room of One's Own* (1929).

g. **George Lucas** (1944–): American filmmaker; creator of *Star Wars* (1977), the largest-selling movie in history.

ANSWER KEY

UNIT 1
GETTING ACQUAINTED

II. Reading for Writing
A. General Understanding (page 3)

(Answers will vary.)

1. He was an old man dressed entirely in black. He had a strong face with a mouth that seemed cruel. He had a high forehead; very large, bushy eyebrows; a mouth with white, sharp teeth; pointed ears; and a very pale, white face. He also had hands that were as cold as ice.

2. He wants to practice speaking English with Harker.

B. Words and Ideas
3. Famous People (page 4)

1. d   2. a   3. b   4. c   5. e

III. Prewriting Activities
3. Forming *Wh-* Questions (pages 6–7)

3. How big is your family?

4. Where do you work?

5. What are your hobbies?

6. What do you do on weekends?

7. What is your favorite book or movie?

8. Why do you like this book or movie?

IV. Structured Writing Focus
D. Editing the Second Draft
1. Adverbs and Expressions of Frequency (page 11)

2. Eduardo is always nervous about speaking English.

3. Alexander never eats American food.

4. Ilana plays tennis twice a week.

5. Hyun-Jin is often homesick on the weekend.

6. Stavros sometimes tells the truth.

2. Proofreading Practice (pages 12–13)

Republic, (The third line incorrectly starts with a comma.), he **has**, **in** September, month**s**

Chinese, years, count**r**ies, sisters, works, **on** 42nd, English, likes, **M**ay, day**s**

UNIT 2
WHO IS A HERO?

II. Reading for Writing
A. General Understanding (page 17)

1. b
2. c
3. b
4. c
5. a
6. c

B. Words and Ideas
A Mother's Story (page 18)

1. flipped
2. explode
3. crawl
4. rural
5. recall
6. wounds
7. wreck
8. perseverance

IV. Structured Writing Focus
B. Preparing the First Draft
2. Choosing a Topic Sentence and a Concluding Sentence (pages 22–23)

topic sentence: b

topic sentence: c

concluding sentence: c

D. Editing the Second Draft
1. The Connectors *and* and *but* (pages 25–26)

1. but   2. and   3. and   4. but

2. King wanted to hate every white person, **but** his father told him he must love instead of hate.

3. He protested with nonviolent marches, **and** he established the Southern Christian Leadership Conference in order to organize these demonstrations.

4. Many people were pleased when King won the Nobel Peace Prize, **but** his ideas weren't accepted by some violent civil rights activists.

5. Martin Luther King lived for peace, but a violent act caused his death.

Count and Noncount Nouns (pages 27–28)

Count:
deeds, people*, projects, scholarships

Noncount:
courage, help, money, perseverance, happiness, knowledge

*people: plural form of *person*

Oprah's Projects (pages 28–29)

1. many
2. a great deal of
3. fifty
4. Many
5. little
6. a few
7. a great deal of
8. a lot of
9. a little
10. much
11. lots of
12. a great deal of

UNIT 3
WEATHERING THE STORM

II. Reading for Writing
A. General Understanding (page 33)

1. watch 2. warning 3. evacuation

Hurricane Watch: Prepare the car; listen to the radio; board up the windows; store water; clear the yard.

Hurricane Warning: Stay away from windows; listen to the radio; put valuable things away.

Hurricane Evacuation: Take emergency supplies; get out; turn off electricity and water.

B. Words and Ideas
Letter to an Insurance Company (page 34)

1. evacuate
2. shelter
3. store
4. waterproof
5. flooded
6. unplug
7. appliances

III. Prewriting Activities
1. Giving and Explaining Instructions (pages 35–36)

(Answers will vary.)

2. Board up the windows. You should board up your windows so that the glass will not break and cut you.

3. Bring in outdoor furniture or tie it down. You should bring in outdoor furniture or tie it down so that it will not blow away.

4. Put gas in the car. You should put gas in the car so that you will be ready to drive away if a hurricane comes to your area.

5. Listen to the radio for instructions. You should listen to the radio to find out how, when, and where to evacuate to a safe place.

IV. Structured Writing Focus
D. Editing the Second Draft
1. Review of Imperatives and Modals
Instructions for the Washing Machine (page 42)

1. should study
2. should empty
3. shouldn't mix
4. must pour
5. can use
6. Do not overload

2. Some Adverbs of Frequency with Imperatives and Modals
How to Be a Good Husband (page 43)

2. **Always love** the woman you marry at least as much as you love yourself.
3. correct
4. You should **frequently share** your feelings with each other.
5. **Never be afraid** to open up to each other.
6. correct
7. Disagreements about money **can often destroy** a marriage.
8. Finally, **never criticize** her mother!

UNIT 4
THE BABY JESSICA CASE

II. Reading for Writing
A. General Understanding (page 47)
The correct order of events:

1. Jessica is born.
2. Cara gives up Jessica for adoption.
3. Jessica goes to live with the DeBoers.
4. Cara and Dan get married.
5. Cara and Dan have another little girl together.
6. The courts must decide who gets Jessica.

III. Prewriting Activities
3. Opinion Letter (page 50)

1. gave up
2. adoptive parents
3. suburb
4. take care of
5. lied
6. birth parents

IV. Structured Writing Focus
A. Starting to Write
Brainstorming (page 52)
(Answers will vary.)

If Jessica remains with the DeBoers,
> she will live with the only parents she has ever known.
>
> she will have her own room.
>
> she will grow up near Ann Arbor, Michigan.

If Jessica goes to live with the Schmidts,
> she will be with her birth parents.
>
> she will grow up in Iowa.
>
> she will have a full-time mother at home.

B. Preparing the First Draft
1. Giving Several Reasons (page 53)
(Answers will vary.)

2. The government saves money because it has fewer orphans to take care of.
3. Society as a whole benefits because children with loving families become better citizens.

3. Practice with Opinions
Opinions (page 54)

Only choices *a* and *b* are clear opinions. Choice *c* is a statement about someone's personal experience, but it isn't an opinion. Choice *d* doesn't express a clear opinion.

Support (page 54)

Choices *c* and *e* do not support the opinion "I disagree with adoption."

Organizing Reasons for Support (page 54)

the individual person: f

the family: a, d, g

society as a whole: b

Using Logical Organizers (page 55)
(*Answers will vary.*)

In addition, the family inheritance could be given away to outsiders. **Also,** the family can never know the child's full medical history. **Finally,** a well-ordered society needs clear blood ties.

D. Editing the Second Draft
1. Subject-Verb Agreement (pages 58–59)

3. The DeBoers work

4. Baby Jessica has lived

5. The Schmidts want

6. ✓

7. ✓

8. We know

It takes a lot of courage for a mother to give up her child for adoption. She doesn't do this because she lacks love for the child she carried in her womb. She <u>does</u> this because she <u>doesn't</u> think she is capable of giving her child everything a baby <u>deserves</u>. Giving up her child for adoption is truly an act of love.

Unfortunately, many children who learn that they <u>were</u> adopted feel unhappy and abandoned. Even though they may <u>have</u> wonderful adoptive families, they cannot forget what their mothers did. They spend their lives looking for their birth mothers. When they finally find them, they often <u>realize</u> that their true parents <u>are</u> the ones who raised them and taught them to love life.

2. The Present Real Conditional (pages 60–61)

1. sends

2. lives, will get

3. will be, lose

4. changes, will experience

5. won't want

UNIT 5
THE GREATEST INVENTION OF THE 20TH CENTURY

II. Reading for Writing
A. General Understanding (page 65)

1918; Eco's grandfather; the Spanish flu; he died.

1972; Eco; a sickness like the Spanish flu; he was cured.

1. F   2. F   3. T   4. T

B. Words and Ideas
2. The Discovery of Penicillin (page 66)

2. f   3. b   4. c   5. e   6. a

1. thanks to

2. Within

3. Instead of

4. Although

5. Despite

6. so

III. Prewriting Activities
Inventions (page 67)
1. These are all inventions of the 19th century.

IV. Structured Writing Focus
B. Preparing the First Draft
The Advantages of Old Age (page 70)
Sentences that belong: a, c, d, e, f, g, i

Possible concluding sentence: I look forward to living to a very old age in order to be with my family and to discover new things about the world.

D. Editing the Second Draft
1. Superlative Forms of Adjectives
Paper and Printing (page 73)
the best evidence, the biggest mistake, the largest contribution, the best system, one of the highest achievements

2. Gerunds and Infinitives
Can You Imagine? (pages 75–77)
2. watching
3. receiving
4. becoming
5. to do
6. to study / studying
7. to become
8. to work
9. to trust
10. studying
11. to question
12. making

14. communicating
15. doing
16. to do
17. working
18. to get
19. understanding

20. to give
21. proving
22. dreaming

UNIT 6
HOME SWEET HOME

II. Reading for Writing
A. General Understanding (page 81)
Loomis Street: 4, 11, 12

Mango Street: 5, 8, 9, 13, 14

Ideal House: 2, 3, 6, 7, 10

III. Prewriting Activities
A. Describing Shapes and Designs
1. Using Prepositions (page 83)
1. below/under
2. above/over
3. close to/near/next to
4. In the upper right-hand corner
5. close to
6. Below/Under
7. inside

IV. Structured Writing Focus
D. Editing the Second Draft
1. *There Is/There Are*
A Visual Analysis of the Room (page 91)
2. there are
3. There is
4. There is
5. There are
6. there is
7. There is
8. there is

2. Noun and Adjective Word Forms (page 92)

Nouns:
intimacy, comfort, color, beauty, space

Adjectives:
beautiful, intimate, colorful, tasteful, spacious

2. space

3. intimate

4. colorful

5. comfortable

6. taste

3. *Feel* and *Look* (page 93)

1. freedom

2. airiness

3. sad

4. peaceful

5. neat

6. clean

7. warm

UNIT 7
A MOUSE GOES TO PARIS

II. Reading for Writing
A. General Understanding (page 97)

1. F   2. T   3. F

(Answers will vary.)

1. most Europeans wanted "American breakfasts" of bacon and eggs.

2. the busiest day was Monday and not enough workers had been hired for Monday.

3. no alcohol was allowed.

4. most chose to stay in Paris hotels.

B. Words and Ideas
2. Reading Between the Lines (page 98)

1. First of all, Norway would have been too far away for people from southern Europe, and Italy would have been too far away for people from northern Europe. In addition, Paris is a city that many people want to go to because it is an important cultural center.

2. The French government wanted its economy to benefit from a European Disney theme park.

3. French intellectuals dislike American culture because they think it is too superficial and too commercialized. They want to protect French culture from American imperialism.

4. Hong Kong was a good choice because Disney can reach the Chinese market, attract Asian tourism, and benefit from Hong Kong's English-speaking tradition.

III. Prewriting Activities
Business Practices Around the World
1. Our Poll (page 99)

In U.S. Business Culture

1. a   2. b   3. a   4. a   5. b

IV. Structured Writing Focus
Memo (page 101)

1. Dan Smith, Transportation Manager, wrote the memo to the CEO of Euro-Disney, Paris.

2. "Re: Trains to Euro-Disney" at the top of the memo shows the topic.

3. Euro-Disney is losing money because some customers do not want to take the trains, which are crowded and uncomfortable at the busiest times.

4. Put more trains in service. Have more employees who speak other languages.

B. Preparing the First Draft
1. Using Connectors to Show Cause and Effect (pages 102–103)

1. The trains to Euro-Disney are very crowded; **therefore,** more trains should be put in service during peak hours.

2. Some people hesitate to plan a trip to the Euro-Disney theme park **because** they don't speak French.

3. There will be additional trains going to the Euro-Disney station; **therefore,** people will feel more comfortable traveling there by train.

4. There will be more people speaking English, Spanish, Italian, and German at train stations on the line to Euro-Disney; **therefore,** more tourists will be able to find their way around.

5. Euro-Disney expects more people to come to their theme park **because** they are making travel arrangements easier.

3. Using the Appropriate Tone (page 104)

Acceptable: a, c, f, g

Not appropriate: b, d, e

D. Editing the Second Draft
1. Infinitive of Purpose (pages 105–106)

(Answers will vary.)

1. Disney has very strict work rules **in order to make sure** its employees work hard.

2. Euro-Disney served French customers croissants and coffee for breakfast **in order to make** them feel comfortable and welcome at the theme park.

3. Business people should study other cultures **in order to understand** the people they want to do business with.

2. Verb Tense Logic
Disney Goes to Hong Kong (page 107)

takes → took

will improve ✓

came → will come

will be ✓

had → has

will get ✓

are ✓

became → will become

was → will be

UNIT 8
THE CRIME THAT DIDN'T HAPPEN

II. Reading for Writing
A. General Understanding
Comparing Two Stories (pages 111–112)

(Answers will vary.)

1. Both John Coppola and Jacqueline Loreau lost something valuable.

2. Ms. Loreau got her money back, but Mr. Coppola has still not found his violin.

3. The Belgian tourist lost $10,000 in cash; however, Mr. Coppola lost his $50,000 violin.

4. In both stories, the police were involved.

5. A reward was offered by both Ms. Loreau and Mr. Coppola.

III. Prewriting Activities
A. Reading Newspapers
1. Where Can You Find It? (page 115)

1. a

2. b, e

3. i

4. b

5. f

6. c

7. g

8. d

9. h

10. e

11. a

12. f

13. h

14. f

2. Headlines and Articles (page 116)

1. The police catch a thief after a big chase downtown.

2. A woman saves a child from a burning building. The police arrest a suspect.

3. There is a trade conference in Geneva.

4. A dog rescues a teen.

5. The parents are inside; the baby is outside.

a. 3   b. 4   c. 5   d. 1   e. 2

IV. Structured Writing Focus

D. Editing the Second Draft

1. Articles

Recognizing the Need for an Article (page 120)

a gun, a verdict, a knife, a man, a judge, a law, a lawyer

A Close Call (page 121)

1. an

2. The

3. a

4. the

5. the

6. ✗

7. the

8. A

9. the

10. ✗

A Close Call (continued, page 122)

11. The

12. a

13. the

14. a

15. the

16. the

17. the

18. the

19. the

20. a

2. Nouns and Determiners (pages 122–123)

each laws → all laws

another people → other people

this two extreme positions → these two extreme positions

These reasons ✓

every men and women → every man and woman

all child → all children

UNIT 9
FABLES FOR OUR TIME

II. Reading for Writing

A. General Understanding

1. The Traditional Story

Little Red Riding Hood (page 128)

Chain of events: Red Riding Hood's mother told her to take some food to her grandmother, but not to leave the path. → Red Riding Hood met the wolf and answered his questions. → Red Riding Hood picked flowers. → The wolf killed the grandmother. → The wolf dressed up in the grandmother's clothes. → Red Riding Hood went to her grandmother's house. → Red Riding Hood didn't recognize the wolf. → The wolf tried to kill Red Riding Hood, but a hunter killed him.

Characters: the wolf, her grandmother, the hunter

2. The Modern Story
The Little Girl and the Wolf (page 129)

Chain of events: A wolf waited for a girl. → A girl finally came along.→ The girl talked to the wolf and answered his questions. → The wolf went away. → The wolf killed the grandmother. → The girl recognized the wolf in her grandmother's clothes. → The girl killed the wolf.

Time: the present

Characters: the girl and the wolf

III. Prewriting Activities
B. Animals in Folktales
Dances with Wolves (page 132)

(Answers will vary.)

2. Don't eat your food so fast!
3. He is "hungry" for women and is always trying to take advantage of them.
4. He looks nicer than he is.
5. Pretend you need help when you don't.

IV. Structured Writing Focus
What Is an Update? (pages 133–134)

Matching Folktales

1. c   2. a   3. b

D. Editing the Second Draft
1. Practice with the Simple Past Tense
Beauty and the Beast (pages 137–138)

spends → spent

taked → took

begs → begged

told ✓

had arrived → arrived

eats → ate

hears → heard

go → went

meets → met

began ✓

hurried ✓

say → said

turns → turned

2. Time Clauses (pages 138–140)

1. a   2. b   3. b   4. b

2. After Beauty took the time to understand the Beast, she fell in love with him.

Beauty fell in love with the Beast after she took the time to understand him.

3. While Beauty was away from the Beast, she realized her true feelings.

Beauty realized her true feelings while she was away from the Beast.

4. After the Beast learned to be gentle and patient, he was ready to get married.

The Beast was ready to get married after he learned to be gentle and patient.

5. When Beauty learned to judge the Beast by his goodness, she was ready for marriage.

Beauty was ready for marriage when she learned to judge the Beast by his goodness.

3. Prepositions of Place (pages 140–141)

"Moon Princess"

3. on → in
4. through → in
5. on ✓
6. on → in

7. from
8. on

9. in

10. to

11. out

12. in

4. Quotations (pages 141–142)

2. "Dearest Beast, you must be strong and live so that we can be husband and wife," said Beauty.

3. The Moon Princess said, "I must leave you on that night."

4. "Too soon," she said.

5. The kind parents said, "We will hire a thousand samurai to protect you."

UNIT 10
WHAT I HAVE LIVED FOR

II. Reading for Writing

A. General Understanding (page 147)

1. T   2. T   3. F   4. T   5. T

B. Words and Ideas

1. Explaining the Meaning (pages 147–148)

(Answers will vary.)

1. Love and knowledge help people understand heaven.

2. Russell's pity for others' pain always helped him remember he lives on earth, not in heaven.

3. Russell wanted to understand men's hearts because he wished to know more about human emotions.

4. He can't stop all the evils he sees in society because they are so widespread.

IV. Structured Writing Focus

B. Preparing the First Draft

2. Thesis Statement (pages 153–154)

2. 5 paragraphs (introduction, 3 body paragraphs, conclusion)

Topics: family life, self-confidence, education

3. 3 paragraphs (introduction, 1 body paragraph, conclusion)

Topic: good parenting

D. Editing the Second Draft

1. The Present Perfect Tense (pages 156–157)

1. have understood

2. have helped

3. has suffered

4. have found

5. have become

learned, knew, have taught, have guided, see, have always tried

2. Future Time Clauses (page 158)

2. find, will be

3. happens, will disappear

4. will feel, am

3. Word Forms (pages 159–161)

Adverbs:
gladly, helplessly, overwhelmingly, terribly, unbearably

suffered, terrible, victim, unbearable, overwhelmingly, relief, victimized, alleviate, suffering, gladly